KV-577-499

Television
The first forty years
Anthony Davis

Also available in this series:

Television:
Behind the screen
Peter Fairley

Television:
Here is the news
Anthony Davis

Television
The first forty years

Anthony Davis

A
TVTimes
Book

Independent Television Publications Ltd, London

Independent Television Publications Ltd
247 Tottenham Court Road
London W1P 0AU

© Anthony Davis 1976

ISBN: 0 900 72757 8

Filmset in 'Monophoto' Times 10 on 11 pt by
Richard Clay (The Chaucer Press), Ltd, Bungay, Suffolk
and printed in Great Britain by
Fletcher & Son Ltd, Norwich

This book shall not, by way of
trade or otherwise, be lent, re-sold,
hired out or otherwise circulated
without the publisher's prior
consent in any form of binding
or cover other than that in which
it is published and without a
similar condition including this
condition being imposed on the
subsequent purchaser. The book
is published at a net price and
is supplied subject to the
Publishers Association Standard
Conditions of Sale registered
under the Restrictive Trade
Practices Act, 1956.

Contents

Foreword

Television has overtaken trains and cars, and it is right up with the weather – as the main subject of people's casual conversation. Yet it isn't, in fact, an *easy* subject. Considered in one way, it is a range of very different experiences – sport, humour, argument, news, travel; the single set is theatre, shopwindow, gallery, cinema, nursery, lecture room; and no one viewer, or critic, is well equipped to speak of all these. Considered in another way, it is a single experience more widely shared than any other; and this provokes sharp reactions about other people's tastes and lifestyles – even though it may in the end increase our tolerance and understanding, by giving us broader company in our own home than we should ever seek for ourselves.

It is wholly good that television, often enjoyed and often guiltily decried, should be the starting-point of much talk; for its task is to rouse as well as soothe, to enrich lives as well as sweeten leisure. But worthwhile talk must have a basis of fact, if comments on the deceptively simple picture and the questions it raises are not to miss the point. That is why I welcome warmly this background book, timed to coincide with the fortieth birthday of television and the twenty-first birthday of ITV. I hope that many will read it, keep it on their sets, and even refer to it before writing to broadcasters and asking the impossible; it may not continue to be the perfect viewers' *vade mecum* throughout the next 21 years, but it will certainly be, for a good while yet, the most useful of general guides to the scene beyond the screen.

Brian Young

Director General
Independent Broadcasting Authority

15th April, 1976

Introduction

Television is Britain's most popular pastime. Nearly half the population spend most of their leisure time viewing, and the average individual watches for 19 hours 27 minutes a week.* In the average home that can receive both BBC and ITV programmes (and there are 18 million such homes) the set is on for 5·2 hours a day, 2·9 of them tuned to ITV.†

Much money is involved. Between them, the BBC and ITV spend some £200 million a year on providing programmes. The public spend millions on buying and renting newer and better receivers.

When television began in 1936 it filled only a dozen hours a week, while from 1972 it has been available for more than 100 hours a week and the choice of programmes between the three channels is wide. At first it was simply a medium of entertainment; today (in the words of Sir Robert Fraser, who was the chief architect of ITV) it is theatre and newspaper in one. Listening to some critics, of course, one might think that television consisted principally of quiz shows, wrestling and soap operas, but that is no more true than to suggest that its main output is of current affairs, arts and educational programmes. In fact, they are all part of television today.

This book looks at many facets of television and tells the story of its development since 1936. It incorporates information gained from many people over many years, from administrators, programme producers and performers alike. I am grateful to them all.

A.D.

* *BBC Annual Report*, 1976.
† JICTAR figures, *ITV 1976*.

Chapter 1

The growth of television

BBC Television, the world's first regular service, began at 3 p.m. on 2 November 1936. It was not front page news, but then there had been trial transmissions earlier in the year from the Radio Show at Olympia, and anyway the number of sets available to receive the new service was less than 400 and the range of the transmitter was only 30 miles.

The announcement that introduced the new service was read by Leslie Mitchell, formerly a radio announcer, who, according to the publicity material, had been chosen as senior television announcer from 590 handsome young men. His pay was £7 a week. The opening speech was by Major G. C. Tryon, the Postmaster General, and at 3.15 there was an interval. (There were to be plenty of intervals in the early days to avoid the danger of eye strain among viewers – or lookers, gazers, watchers, visionists, witnesses and teleseers as they were variously known.) This was followed by a cinema newsreel, and variety with musical comedy star Adele Dixon, Buck and Bubbles (coloured American comedy dancers) and the Lai Founs (Chinese jugglers). At 4 p.m. the service closed down until 9 o'clock.

The evening's viewing consisted of *Television Comes to London*, a BBC film showing the interior of Alexandra Palace, headquarters of the new service. At 9.20 there was *Picture Page*, a magazine programme that was to create television's first 'personality' in Canadian actress Joan Miller, who appeared as a switchboard girl to connect viewers with the famous. The famous in the first edition were Jim Mollison, the airman, Kay Stammers, the tennis player, and Bossy Phelps, the royal bargemaster, who were interviewed by Jasmine Bligh and John Snagge. After another showing of the newsreel the programme ended at 10 p.m.

The rest of the week brought a display by champion alsatian dogs, a bus driver showing a model he had built of Drake's ship, *The Golden Hind*, variety with Bebe Daniels and Ben Lyon, the BBC Dance Orchestra conducted by Henry Hall, demonstrations of tap dancing and boxing, a ballet, a programme on prize chrysanthemums, scenes from *Marigold* (a West End play starring Sophie Stewart), a zoo programme with David Seth Smith, cabaret with ventriloquist Arthur Prince and Jim, a programme on pictures and sculptures being exhibited in London, and two more showings of the film *Television Comes to London.*

There was one hour in the afternoon and one hour in the evening – and no television on Sundays. Cecil Madden, the programme organiser and senior producer, had a budget of £1,000 a week for all his programmes.

Television's first big occasion was the Coronation of George VI in May 1937. Cameras were not allowed in Westminster Abbey but three were installed on the processional route at Hyde Park Corner, and an eight-mile cable linked a portable transmitter in a four-ton lorry with Alexandra Palace. Freddie Grisewood was the commentator. Several thousand people watched the television coverage, crowding round sets in the homes of pioneer owners, some, it was reported, in places as far as sixty miles away, and when Queen Mary, the new King's mother, smiled directly at the audience it was regarded as a triumph.

But the sale of sets was still slow. By the end of 1937 there were only 2,000 in use. In February 1938 television opened for an hour on Sundays, but Madden had many problems. Artists were wary of the new medium and impresarios were reluctant to make them available. The Jockey Club, the British Boxing Board of Control and other sporting authorities did not welcome television cameras either.

However, sales continued to rise gradually as sets dropped in price from £60 to between £25 and £40 for a ten-inch screen. There were 5,000 in use by the end of 1938 and 20,000 by 1 September 1939, when, two days before the outbreak of the Second World War, television was closed down for the war's duration in case German bombers should home on the transmitter. No announcement was made. Television had extended into the mornings for an hour for transmissions from the 1939 Radiolympia Show under the slogan and title, *Come and Be Televised.* At noon there was a showing of a Mickey Mouse cartoon. When it ended the screen went blank. Television's first era was over.

The post-war period

Television re-opened on 7 June 1946 from the same headquarters at Alexandra Palace and one of the first programmes was an outside broadcast of the Victory Parade. That night Leslie Mitchell compered variety, Margot Fonteyn danced and George More O'Ferrall produced Shaw's *Dark Lady of the Sonnets.*

There were still fewer than 100,000 viewers, all necessarily in the London area because of the limited range of the transmitter. But only three other countries, America, Russia and France, had television. There was an hour in the afternoon and ninety minutes in the evening, both on weekdays and Sundays.

The first week brought Fred Streeter in the garden at Alexandra Palace, the Hogarth Puppet Theatre for children, Robert Eddison and Margaret Rutherford in *The Importance of Being Earnest*, Harry Roy and his band, a demonstration of heavyweight wrestling, French singer Sylvie Saint-Clair, and Edwardian music hall from the Player's Theatre with Leonard Sachs as chairman and a cast including Hattie Jacques. Sylvia Peters and Macdonald Hobley were new announcers.

In December 1949 a second transmitter opened at Sutton Coldfield in the Midlands and the number of set owners rose to 344,000. Richard Dimbleby was a new star, introducing programmes from the British Museum and the Royal Mint and, on 27 August 1950, the first live television from the other side of the Channel, *Calais en Fête*, transmitted by the 100-year-old submarine cable between the two countries.

In 1951 a third transmitter opened in the Manchester area, followed a year later by transmitters in Scotland; 80 per cent of the population were now within reach of television. Licence holders rose to two millions as *What's My Line?* established grouchy Gilbert Harding as television's first superstar, but the industry still needed something to stimulate sales. They got it in the Coronation.

The BBC had sought permission well in advance to screen the Coronation service but it had been refused. Peter Dimmock, who was

What's My Line? with Isobel Barnett, Ted Moult, Sara Leighton and Gilbert Harding

to be in charge of the arrangements, argued the case with a demonstration in Westminster Abbey proving that the lights required would not be excessive and that the cameras need not be obtrusive, and eventually the decision was reversed.

The Coronation was to be television's longest broadcast up to that time, from 10 in the morning, when Sylvia Peters in the studio introduced Berkeley Smith, the commentator outside Buckingham Palace, to 11.30 that night when Richard Dimbleby, the commentator in the Abbey, said farewell. The day was a personal triumph for Dimbleby and a triumph also for television. A million new aerials had gone up for the occasion. Britons had crowded into public halls and the homes of friends to watch, and the programme had also been received in France, Germany, Holland and Belgium in the beginnings of Eurovision. In Britain alone an estimated twenty million people saw some part of it.

The broadcast changed attitudes to television. Its right to be present on major public occasions was established and the eminent came to accept it, if not to welcome it. In the following year the sale of sets rose by 50 per cent, though *Radio Times* still printed television programmes at the back of the magazine. Even that was about to change.

The Coronation – the state coach passes a television camera on its way to Westminster Abbey

ITV is born

Conservative MP Selwyn Lloyd was one of the first to propose ending the BBC's monopoly in television. He made a minority report dissenting from the main Beveridge Committee report on Broadcasting in 1949, suggesting that television should be handed over to a commercially sponsored corporation licensed by a British Broadcasting Commission. Support came from Norman Collins, Controller of BBC Television since 1947, who resigned, complaining that the BBC hierarchy were either apathetic or actually hostile to the younger medium. He believed that television must eventually outstrip radio in popularity and began making speeches advocating commercial television.

In January 1951 the Beveridge Committee rejected the idea of sponsored television and the Labour government accepted their view. But in October Labour were ousted and Churchill and the Conservatives – dedicated to free and competitive enterprise – returned to power. Furthermore, they were smarting at the coverage that had been given to the Attlee government by the BBC, which they felt had been biased to the left.

The television controversy hotted up. The Labour Party termed the prospect of commercial television 'a national disaster'. The Archbishop of York said that it should be resisted 'for the sake of our children'. Labour MP Christopher Mayhew was one of the founders of the National Television Council, whose members campaigned against commercial television with alarming stories of the Philistinism and commercialism of sponsored broadcasting in America. On the other side, the Popular Television Association, backed by set manufacturers, the advertising industry and Tory MPs, campaigned for 'people's television', deriding BBC programmes as cosy, nannyish and low-budget.

Churchill insisted that there had to be competition, and in November 1953 the government issued a memorandum of television policy that led, after a Parliamentary battle, to the Television Act of 1954, which set up the Independent Television Authority under Sir Kenneth (now Lord) Clark, Chairman of the Arts Council, to provide an alternative service for ten years. The word 'commercial' was buried in favour of the less emotive 'independent', and sponsorship on the American pattern was ruled out; advertisers in Britain would be allowed merely to buy time as they bought space in newspapers.

The ITA devised a federal, regional structure for ITV, erected the first transmitter and appointed the first programme-making companies; the companies recruited staff and built studios in a remarkably short space of time and ITV opened on 22 September 1955.

Like the BBC it began transmitting in London only and could reach only 190,000 homes when the first programmes went out. It opened with a ceremony televised from London's Guildhall at 7.15 p.m. There were speeches by the Lord Mayor, Sir Seymour Howard; by Sir Kenneth Clark; and by the Postmaster General, Dr Charles Hill, later (as Lord Hill) to be chairman successively of both the ITA and the BBC. This was followed at 8 p.m. by *Variety*, with an all-star bill including Billy Cotton, Shirley Abicair, Reg Dixon, John Hanson and Harry Secombe. At 8.40 Robert Morley introduced snippets from three plays, one of them being *The Importance of Being Earnest* with Dame Edith Evans and Sir John Gielgud. At 9.10 there was *Professional Boxing*, at 10 p.m. the *News*, and at 10.15 a fashion show from a West End hotel, introduced by Leslie Mitchell, who had introduced the first BBC Television programmes. The last programme was *Cabaret* at 10.30 with Billy Ternent's Orchestra.

A leader in the first issue of the original ITV programme journal *TV Times* declared,

> So far television in this country has been a monopoly restricted by limited finance and often, or so it seemed, restricted by a lofty attitude towards the wishes of viewers by those in control. That situation has now undergone a great and dramatic change. Viewers will no longer have to accept what has been deemed best for them. They will be able to pick and choose. And the new Independent Television programme planners aim at giving viewers what viewers want – at the times viewers want it.

What viewers got was typified by the *News*, more visual and colloquial than anything provided by the BBC. The other key elements were all there in the first week's viewing. There were top American shows such as *I Love Lucy*, a domestic comedy series starring Lucille Ball, and *Dragnet*, a cops and robbers series with Jack Webb as Police Sergeant Joe Friday. It was the first time programmes like these had been seen in Britain.

There were quiz shows with cash prizes for the winners, the first two being Hughie Green's *Double Your Money* and Michael Miles's *Take Your Pick*, both based on successful Radio Luxembourg programmes. There was big-name variety, typified by *Sunday Night at the London Palladium*, which had Gracie Fields as its first star, and incorporated a weekly games interlude in which Tommy Trinder, the first compere, induced honeymoon couples to bounce balls, burst balloons and hurl hoops for more prizes. For children there was *The Adventures of Robin Hood*, starring Richard Greene, and destined to become one of television's all-time successes.

And programmes *were* at the times viewers wanted them. The BBC had been showing serious and minority-interest programmes in the middle of the evening, so that peak time might be devoted to a play,

I Love Lucy, *with William Frawley, Vivian Vance, Lucille Ball and Desi Arnaz*

A scene from Robin Hood *with Richard Greene (left) as the outlaw leader*

an opera or a visit to a glassworks. ITV followed the American system of screening programmes with mass audience appeal at peak time and relegating programmes of lesser appeal – and the schedules did contain some – to earlier or later slots. The same popular shows were to be in the same time slots week after week, establishing a more regular, familiar pattern than the BBC had offered.

The people liked the pattern, but the path of the first programme companies was not paved with gold. They had to exist on advertising revenue and advertisers were wary of spending £1,000 a minute while coverage was still so small. Revenue dropped from £100,000 in the first month to £74,000 in December and £59,000 in January 1956.

In February 1956 ITV expanded to the Midlands (following the same route as the BBC had done earlier) and revenue rose to £80,000, but the ITV companies were to lose £11 million in the first eighteen months of operation. It was spring 1957 before they began to break even, and then began the progress that was to lead to the declaration by Roy (later Lord) Thomson of Scottish Television that a licence to operate a television station was a licence to print money.

At the end of 1957 television licences exceeded radio licences for the first time, 7·5 million for television and 7·1 million for radio, and the Queen gave royal recognition to this fact by making her first Christmas Day broadcast on television.

Out of 539 programmes that had been listed in London's Top Ten chart since the start of ITV, 536 had been ITV's.* With its network nearing completion, ITV was watched, on average, by more than 70 per cent of the audience who had a choice. And then came Pilkington.

Pilkington and BBC2

Not everyone was happy with the ITV programmes. In 1960 a special committee to consider the future of broadcasting was set up under the chairmanship of glass manufacturer Sir Harry Pilkington, and when it reported in 1962 it exploded a bomb under ITV. The report had mainly praise for the BBC. 'The BBC know good broadcasting . . . by and large they are providing it.' It had frowns for ITV. 'Dissatisfaction with television can largely be ascribed to the independent television service . . . there is much that lacks quality.'†

ITV was disconcerted, but so was the government, which rejected the main Pilkington proposal – that the ITA should sell the advertising, plan the schedules and use the companies merely as programme providers. ITV's response was to broaden the range of its programmes. In 1956 the ITA had classified 19 per cent of ITV programmes (totalling 9·5 hours a week) as 'serious'; by 1963 they totalled

* TAM figures.
† *Report of the Committee on Broadcasting* (HMSO).

24 hours, representing 37 per cent, and were still increasing. Meanwhile a special levy was introduced on advertising revenue to trim the profits of the ITV companies, and the third channel which had become available was awarded to the BBC.

Publicity for the channel began in 1963, using as symbols two kangaroos named Hullaballoo and Custard. Promotion for what was the first new television service in Britain for nine years was massive. It opened on 20 April 1964 and was a disaster. The scheduled opening programmes were the comedy group *The Alberts* at 7.30 p.m., followed by the musical *Kiss Me Kate* with Patricia Morrison and Howard Keel at 8 p.m., Russian comic Arkady Ralkin with the Leningrad Miniature Theatre Company at 9.35 and a firework display from Southend pier at 10.20.

It was not the BBC's fault that a power failure in West London blacked out the opening night but it was an ill omen. Instead of simply scheduling drama on BBC2 against light entertainment on BBC1 or a documentary on 2 against a Western on 1, Michael Peacock, the first Controller, had devised what was called the Seven Faces of the Week to provide alternative viewing. Each night on BBC2 had a different character. Monday night meant light entertainment; Tuesday night, education; Wednesday night, repeats; Thursday night, minority-interest programmes; Friday night, drama. The public did not take to the idea. Rightly or wrongly, it classed BBC2 as a highbrow channel.

A second error was that timings of programmes on the two channels did not coincide. In the first week *Z Cars* began at 8 p.m. on BBC1 when BBC2 was in the middle of a repeat of a four-year-old dramatised crime documentary. Chaplin's *The Gold Rush* began on BBC2 at 8.20 p.m. while BBC1 was still showing *Z Cars*. The *News* on BBC2 had a different time almost every night, 10.35 p.m. on Monday and Tuesday, 10.15 on Wednesday, 10.45 on Thursday, 10 on Friday.

People had to have new or converted sets to receive BBC2, which was transmitted on UHF instead of VHF like BBC1 and ITV, and by June only 90,000 were tuned in. Manufacturers complained that their sets would remain unsold unless the service improved. Peacock scrapped the Seven Faces scheme. 'We will now have a mixed bag of programmes; we will be more in common with other networks,' he told the Press. 'It is all part of growing up.'

In 1965 David Attenborough succeeded Peacock, bringing in more popular drama and more humour, and time junctions were created between BBC1 and 2 so that viewers could make a genuine choice between alternatives. Attenborough moved into new programme areas – among them, foreign films and finance – and launched major series like *The Forsyte Saga* and *The Six Wives of Henry VIII*.

They were hugely successful but did not end criticism of BBC2.

Susan Hampshire and Eric Porter in The Forsyte Saga

Keith Michell as Henry and Rosalie Crutchley as Catherine Parr in The Six Wives of Henry VIII

Many viewers, who wanted to see the programmes, were still unable to receive BBC2 in the areas where they lived, and so the programmes had to be repeated on BBC1 before they had finished their runs on 2. But with series like these and the introduction of colour on BBC2 in 1967 – not available on BBC1 and ITV until 1969 – the channel was established.

Meanwhile, at ITV changes were made when the companies' contracts expired and the ITA allocated new franchises in 1967. The chairman, Lord Hill, announced a major reshuffle. The contractors for Wales and the West were dispossessed and a new consortium appointed in their place. One of ITV's founder companies in London was invited to merge with another company in a minority role if it wanted to remain in ITV. The Northern region was divided to create space for another new company.

New schedules were devised. Long-running series like *Double Your Money* and *Take Your Pick*, favourites with millions of viewers, were discontinued. New and unfamiliar shows replaced them. The changes were too sweeping and too sudden for the public.

It happened as BBC1 hit back hard. Under former newspaperman Sir Hugh Greene, who had become Director General in 1960, the Corporation had set out to win back a fair share of the viewing audience. It had followed ITV's tactics in slotting popular programmes at peak times, programmes like *Maigret*, *Perry Mason*, *Dr. Finlay's Casebook*, *Z Cars* and *Steptoe and Son*. The opening of BBC2 gave the Corporation a big advantage because it could pit mass-appeal programmes against ITV on BBC1 and offer an alternative on BBC2 for minority interests. ITV's ratings fell. By 1968 ITV had to accept that its share of the audience had fallen to 55 per cent*; BBC figures put it considerably lower.

Television today

In the seventies the pattern steadied with ITV retaining the major share of the viewing audience, some 56 per cent, BBC1 having 37 per cent and BBC2 about 7 per cent.†

BBC2 had reached most of the country and was capable of winning an audience of 10 million at peak time by showing Western series like *Alias Smith and Jones* on Monday nights when BBC1 was showing *Panorama* and ITV was showing *World in Action*. But it remained a minority channel. Moon walks, international soccer, Miss World contests, heavyweight title fights and other major audience pullers were allocated automatically by the BBC to the first channel.

In the opening years of the seventies television surged forward

* ITV Evidence to the Annan Committee, 1975.
† JICTAR figures.

again. Colour had been introduced on BBC1 and ITV in 1969 and when Chancellor Anthony Barber eased the credit squeeze in a mini-Budget in July 1971, sales of colour sets leapt so rapidly that factories could not meet the demand. By 1975 there were more than 17 million television licences, 10·1 million for monochrome sets and 7·5 million for colour sets. The two-set home was becoming commonplace.

Experiments in cable television, which could give viewers a wider choice of programmes, including locally originated ones, began at Greenwich and four more stations – at Bristol, Swindon, Sheffield and Wellingborough – followed. Video cassette recorders came on the market, making it possible for viewers to record one programme while watching another, or, by setting a time switch, to record a programme while away from home for viewing later.

In 1972 the government swept away restrictions on television's hours of broadcasting. For years the main channels had been limited to 50 hours a week, plus exempt classes including school and religious programmes, party political broadcasts and outside broadcasts (up to a maximum of 350 hours a year) which did not count against the 50 hour maximum.

Pressure from ITV had resulted in a meagre increase to 53·5 hours a week, but with the removal of all restrictions, ITV was able to announce up to 20 extra hours of television on weekdays. The TV day now stretched to 15 hours and plans were discussed for breakfast-time shows. The BBC followed more slowly because, while ITV could hope to recoup the extra costs from additional advertising slots, extra hours meant only extra expense for the BBC.

The start of the seventies also brought increased lobbying for a fourth television channel. ITV sought it in order to compete on equal terms with the BBC. Some wanted to see another commercial channel with a different structure; others wanted it to be devoted to education. In 1974 a Committee of Inquiry into the Future of Broadcasting was set up under the chairmanship of Lord Annan, Provost of University College, London, and the development of British television was frozen to await the Committee's recommendations.

Chapter 2
Technical development

The heart of television is the studio and the BBC and ITV companies have the best equipped studios available. Britain's newest studio complex is that of London Weekend Television, which opened in 1972 on London's South Bank, near the Royal Festival Hall and the National Theatre. It houses five studios ranging in size from Studio One, designed for major light entertainment spectaculars and covering an area of 7,600 square feet, down to a studio of 350 square feet for continuity announcements and weather forecasts.

The three main studios feature a lighting grid thirty feet above floor level with lamps suspended on struts. The lighting control is computerised and 'plots' can be filed in a corestore memory system so that the same arrangement and intensity of lighting may be repeated at will.

The cameras in the studios are all colour models, some mounted on wheeled 'dollies', some on cranes that can carry the cameraman high in the air. Other studio equipment includes microphones (some mounted on the elongated fishing rods called 'booms'), stands for graphics, devices for rolling captions, special effects generators for simulating rain, fog and mist, projector screens for slides and films, and teleprompters from which performers can read scripts while seeming to talk directly to the camera.

In the control suites associated with the studios are videotape recorders (VTR machines), including a slow-motion replay unit and video cassette models, and telecine machines for running films.

Around the studios are technical areas of 17,000 square feet incorporating mechanical workshops, paint and carpenters' shops and a scenic service area of 26,000 square feet including the props department. There are rehearsal rooms, artists' dressing-rooms and wardrobe and make-up departments. Overlooking these areas is a gallery with control points for the Transport Manager, Master Painter, Scenery Master, Electrical Foreman, Property Master and Production Manager and crew rooms for the technical and studio staff.

The traffic flow has been carefully planned. Artists enter from the building's river frontage through a reception area leading to the dressing-rooms, the wardrobe and make-up departments and the studios. Invited audiences enter on the west side through a foyer to a 250-seat gallery of Studio One. Large doors at the east end of the block allow scenery, drapes and props to be brought in for assembly in the scenic area, which also has direct access to the studios.

London Weekend Television's Studio One – view from the gallery

Aerial view of the BBC Television Centre

Outside broadcast signals can be received directly by radio-link equipment into the roof of the adjoining 25-storey 275-foot-high administration offices tower. Co-axial cables and communications circuits link the complex to a Post Office switching centre that connects with the transmitters and other parts of the ITV network.

Since the completion of the South Bank complex, London Weekend has built another centre at Wembley, Middlesex, primarily as the base for its outside broadcast units, but also including a studio of 8,000 square feet for use at peak production times, and a film department of two 16-mm film crews (who contribute to plays and documentaries) with six editing rooms, film libraries and a preview theatre.

And, of course, London Weekend is just one of ITV's fifteen programme companies, although a major one; the BBC Television Centre, which opened in 1960 in West London's Wood Lane, is much bigger, with seven full-scale production studios, the largest of which, Studio One, is 10,800 square feet in area. In addition, the BBC has studios nearby at Lime Grove for current affairs programmes and a Television Theatre at Shepherd's Bush for light entertainment shows, as well as film studios at Ealing.

Both the BBC and ITN have Westminster studios near the Houses of Parliament. These are small remote-controlled studios from which Parliamentary correspondents can be switched into news programmes, all technicalities being handled several miles away in the headquarters.

The first studios

The BBC's first studios were primitive by comparison. When television began at Alexandra Palace in 1936 there were two studios each fifty feet long, but only one was used in any week. One studio housed Baird equipment and the other Marconi–EMI equipment, for television began with a technical competition.

Lord Selsdon's Committee, set up by the Postmaster General to advise him on the development of television, had recommended in 1935 that the BBC should hold a public trial of the rivals, so the Baird and Marconi–EMI systems were used on alternate weeks. They differed fundamentally. A television picture is created by tracing out the scene before the camera in a series of horizontal lines, sub-divided into tiny elements. The light value of each element is scanned and transmitted in sequence from left to right and line by line to be rebuilt at the receiver in accordance with the transmitted signal, the process being fast enough to deceive the eye into thinking it sees all the elements at once.

The system developed by John Logie Baird just met the minimum standard called for by the Selsdon Committee of 240 lines and 25 pictures a second, scanning the subject by mechanical means involving mirrors spaced round a rotating drum. The Marconi–EMI system, in which a major part had been played by Isaac, later Sir Isaac, Shoenberg, scanned electronically by an electron beam. It operated on a standard of 405 lines and used interlaced scanning, sending first the odd lines and then the even ones, so that, although only 25 pictures a second were transmitted, each area of the screen was scanned 50 times.

The 405 lines gave higher definition than Baird's 240 and the interlaced scanning gave less flickering. The Emitron camera of Marconi–EMI could be used both in the studios and outdoors in the Palace gardens – up to a distance of 1,000 feet, which was the length of the extension cable – whereas Baird's camera, requiring a low level of light around the subject, was confined to studio operation.

It was really no contest. In February 1937, after three months of alternating use, the Postmaster General announced that the Baird system was discarded. Britain's television was to be based on 405 lines and 50 frames per second using electronic scanning, and that standard – created by the Emitron camera – though obsolescent now, is still in use in Britain on the monochrome VHF channels alongside the new 625 lines UHF network.

Until the Baird studio was recommissioned for 405 lines operation

Emitron cameras in the BBC's first studio in 1936

in 1938 there was then only one studio in use. By putting cameras in the centre, it was possible to swing them and use both ends of the studio. Curtains allowed a close-up to be taken while the next scene was prepared behind them. Apart from cinema newsreels and the occasional film, all television was transmitted live from that one studio.

There was no viewfinder on the original cameras. The turret camera with a revolving disc offering the choice of several lenses of different focal lengths, and the single zoom lens of variable focal length used universally today, were still to come. The camera had to be moved in for a close-up and back for a long shot or two cameras had to be used. The director in the control room had only one monitor screen, which showed the picture being transmitted; to check the positions of his other cameras he had to peer out of his window. It was amazing what was produced, using the studio and the gardens. After the first major outside broadcast of the Coronation procession on a damp and dismal day in 1937, the Super Emitron camera tube was developed which was more sensitive, and from that point cameras were to go on improving.

When television returned after the war it was still based on the same Alexandra Palace studios and there it remained until 1949 when the BBC opened eight new studios in West London. One had been a variety theatre, the others were converted film studios.

The biggest task however was to spread television to the country, for it was still confined to an area of some thirty miles around London, as it had been before the war. Work began on new high-power transmitters but progress was slow, due to government restrictions on capital expenditure. It was 1949 before television reached the Midlands, 1951 before it reached Manchester. In 1952 it reached Scotland, then Wales and the West Country, and by the time of the Coronation in 1953 the most populated areas of the country had been covered and a four-year plan began to fill in the remaining areas with medium-power transmitters. By the time this was completed ITV had begun, opening in 1955 with a transmitter at Croydon and expanding by the same route that the BBC had gone, only faster. Within three years three-quarters of the population could receive ITV.

Video recording

A development that was to revolutionise television came in 1956 with video recording. Until then programmes that were not on film had to be transmitted live. There were many disadvantages. A live programme could be repeated only by repeating the show. There was no way of stockpiling programmes for future use or of selling programmes to other countries except by the expensive method of filming.

If a star was not available when a programme slot was available he could not be used, and artists who were working in the theatre in the evenings were just not available. Programme directors worked in fear of technical slips such as a microphone or its shadow dipping into view. Actors feared fluffing their lines or drying up. All these things happened.

An actor in a BBC production of *Mourning becomes Electra* gestured and dislodged his false moustache. He had to finish his speech with his face averted from the camera. An actor due to appear in a Priestley play on BBC was taken ill immediately before transmission and since his replacement had no time to learn his lines he had to act with a script in his hands. Tragedy occurred in an *Armchair Theatre* play called *Underground* in 1958 when actor Gareth Jones died on the set during the performance. The rest of the cast were told, when out of camera shot, that he had been taken ill and they had to ad-lib their way through the remaining scenes. There could be no editing to erase mishaps, nor to improve the pace. If an actor was required to end one scene in plus-fours in a saloon bar and reappear in pyjamas in a bedroom, a linking scene without him had to be written to give him time to change and move across the studio floor.

The first ventures in recording programmes were by pointing a film camera at the screen of a high quality monitor set. This system, called Telerecording, was used to record the Coronation in 1953, but it involved loss of quality, it was expensive and there was no way of knowing the result until the film had been processed. Attention turned to magnetic tape as used in sound recording. The main problem was the high speed at which the tape needed to run in order to accommodate the wider range of frequencies of video signals compared with audio signals. Early experiments involved a speed of 250 inches per second, which was not practical.

The breakthrough came from America where there was an additional need for recording because of the time differences between the coasts. The Ampex videotape recorder shown there in 1956 solved the problem by means of revolving recording heads and transverse scanning – using the tape across its width rather than its length. Four recording heads on a drum rotated at 250 revolutions per minute to scan across the centre of a two-inch-wide tape moving along at 15 inches per second. One edge of the tape was used for the sound track and the other for a control track.

There were still problems in editing tape. Cutting and splicing it like film was dangerously imprecise and so editing was avoided as far as possible. Plays were still recorded in sequence as if they were being transmitted live, though breaks could be called and the tape stopped for set and costume changes; the maxim otherwise was to stop the tape and reshoot only for technical mishaps. If an actor got into difficulties with his lines he was expected to get himself out of them. One actor, bound and gagged in a children's adventure serial, nearly suffocated because of his reluctance to call attention to his discomfort and be the cause of reshooting. However, as the quality of videotape recording improved it became possible to edit by re-recording from the original tape to a second tape, merely stopping and restarting the tapes as required for deletions, insertions or transpositions, and now editing can be done electronically.

The bulk of television's output is on tape today. There are few live programmes other than the news, which itself contains tape and film inserts. Taping programmes has made it possible to use studios around the clock. Actors from companies like the National Theatre can record a play in the daytime and appear in the theatre – *and* on television – at night. Visiting foreign stars can be snapped up for a programme to be shown later when scheduling permits. Tape is incorporated in mobile units for outdoor location work and, with instant playback, the director knows how effective his shooting has been before he leaves the scene. Tape has given television a new freedom.

Yet film has not been made obsolete. Film crews can be smaller, film cameras are easily portable and action sequences can be shot in snippets and cut to give a pace hard to equal with continuous action in front of electronic television cameras. Programmes on film are also easier to sell abroad because of its quality.

Colour and 625 lines

Colour television works on the same principles as monochrome, but involves sending three signals (corresponding to the red, green and blue content of a scene) so a colour camera uses three tubes. Today's colour systems are based on the work in America of the National Television System Committee (NTSC) which in 1951 devised a system that could be received equally well in black and white on monochrome sets. Two years later the Federal Communications Commission gave approval for its introduction, but by 1961 only one of America's three main networks was in colour, due partly to the cost of making colour programmes and partly to the cost of colour receivers for the home.

Britain could also have had colour by this time, for the BBC had begun test transmissions in 1955, but there was a complication. Britain was still using the 405 lines standard, which had stemmed from the Emitron in 1936. It was the penalty of being first in the field, for later comers had adopted more lines to give better definition. To go into colour on 405 lines would have meant that Britain would have been committed to that standard for an indefinite period and out of step with everyone else.

In 1961 an international conference in Stockholm allocated frequencies between thirty-six European countries for 4,000 UHF stations. The government decided that colour should wait until BBC2 was introduced on the new UHF frequencies and using 625 lines like the majority of Continental countries. This came about in 1964, although it was promised that the 405 lines VHF services would be retained for many years and, in fact, it is likely to continue into the eighties. In the meantime, viewers wanting BBC2 as well as BBC1 and ITV had to buy dual standard receivers and additional aerials.

But the service was in being and Britain could at last plan for colour. By this time the American NTSC system no longer looked the best. France and Germany had developed variants that offered greater colour tolerance and required less control. The French system was called SECAM (Sequential Colour with Memory) and the German PAL (Phase Alternation Line). British engineers evaluated the systems and PAL seemed the better, but questions of national prestige were involved. For three years the International Radio Consultative Committee met in attempts to reach agreement on a common colour system for Europe. It was hopeless; De Gaulle's France would never agree to using the German or American system, but Switzerland, Italy and the Scandinavian countries were, like Britain, inclined towards PAL.

By 1966 British set manufacturers were pressing for Britain to decide, unilaterally if necessary; otherwise, they said they would not be able to have sets ready for the start of colour on BBC2, scheduled for 1967. Britain plumped for PAL, and most of Europe did the same.

On 1 July 1967 BBC2 screened tennis from Wimbledon in colour and became the first colour service in Europe. It was greeted with acclaim. A critic appearing on BBC2's *Late Night Line-Up* enthused, 'Even bad programmes are good in colour.' David Attenborough, the network's controller, declared, 'Monochrome is just a degraded picture.' Within months almost all BBC2 programmes were in colour.

BBC1 and ITV were also making programmes in colour, even though they could not transmit them in colour. Technicians needed the experience of working in colour; there was also a need to stockpile colour programmes, and they had to be in colour if they were to be sold to America. Many British programmes were seen at this time in colour in America and monochrome in Britain.

Costs of equipping studios for colour were high. Cameras cost up to £25,000 each and videotape machines £70,000 each, but today the 50 studios in the 20 ITV complexes alone have more than 250 colour camera channels, nearly 100 colour videotape recording machines, 100 colour telecine machines and 20 colour outside broadcast units (£300,000 each). A network of new transmitters had also to be built by both the BBC and ITV. They were sited at communal stations, using one mast for both services. Even so, each high-power transmitting station represented an investment of some £250,000 by each channel. (By the mid-seventies it was £350,000.)

In November 1969 BBC1 and ITV were permitted to start colour services on 625 lines UHF, though the service was available only to half the viewers in the country and there were only 200,000 colour sets in use. Now 95 per cent of the country can receive colour and there are more than 7·5 million sets, but the building of UHF stations is still continuing at the rate of 50 a year. Eventually there will be 50 main and 450 relay stations.

International television

The first programme to be sent across the sea from one country to another was in August 1950 when the BBC relayed a show from Calais as part of the celebrations of the centenary of the submarine cable between England and France. For technical reasons that programme could not be seen in France, but in 1952, when Paris was linked with London for the first time, French and British viewers watched a week of French-produced programmes simultaneously.

In the following year the Coronation ceremony was transmitted from London to France, Holland, Belgium and Western Germany, and a year later, when more countries had opened television services, the networks of eight countries linked to form Eurovision.

British viewers saw a live transmission from behind the Iron Curtain for the first time in 1961. It was the triumphant return to Moscow of Major Yuri Gagarin, the world's first spaceman. In return Russians saw the Trooping the Colour ceremony live from London later in the year.

All these programmes were relayed by land lines and microwave radio links. But in 1962 came the launching from Cape Canaveral of Telstar 1, the first satellite capable of relaying television pictures across the world. In 18 minutes 200 million people in 16 European countries saw baseball from Chicago, a Presidential press conference from Washington, the rocket-launching site at Cape Canaveral, scenes from a performance of *Macbeth* in Ontario, the World's Fair at Seattle, the United Nations building in New York and Niagara Falls. On the satellite's next orbit pictures from nine European capitals including London were transmitted to North America, though the end of the programme was lost when Telstar went out of range. Telstar 1 was in line of sight from both sides of the Atlantic for only about 18 minutes on each $2\frac{1}{2}$-hour orbit.

A year later came the first synchronous satellite on such an orbit that it remained stationary over the same point on the earth's surface, and in 1968 viewers throughout the world could see live pictures from the Olympics in Mexico. In 1969 Intelsat III (put into space by the International Telecommunications Satellite Consortium) brought the first direct live exchanges with Japan. The world was open to live television – at a price.

Today, Eurovision's controlling organisation, the European Broadcasting Union, is the world's largest association of professional broadcasting organisations with nearly 100 members in 71 countries and in a year it relays more than 50,000 news items and 500 sports programmes. It has links on the other side of the Iron Curtain with Intervision (OIRT), which has its headquarters in Prague and members including China and the United Arab Republic, and also with the Asian Broadcasting Union (ABU), which has headquarters in Tokyo and members including India and the group of countries Australasia.

One problem that had to be solved along the way towards this international co-operation was the difference in the lines standards used by different countries. Britain was using 405 lines, France 819 and other European countries 625, so that whenever France or Britain were involved in Eurovision, pictures had to be converted from one standard to another. This was first done in 1952 for the pictures from Paris by training a camera operated on the British line standard on the screen of a monitor set working on the French line standard. But quality was lost in scanning the image. Engineers set out to develop equipment in which the signal remained as a waveform without being reconstituted as a picture during the conversion.

In the event, this was not a major problem, which was fortunate because since the introduction of the 625 lines UHF system in Britain all programmes are originated on 625 lines and have to be converted at the transmitters for those viewers who still have 405 lines sets. But a complication arises when the number of frames or field scans per second is different, as it is in America, which uses 60 per second compared to Britain's 50.

The BBC solved the problem with a Field Stores Converter, incorporating some 5,000 transistors and costing over £100,000, which was first used live for the Mexico Olympics in 1968 when pictures came via the satellite at the originating standard of 525 lines and 60 fields per second. They were received at the Post Office station at Goonhilly Down in Cornwall, routed to the TV Centre and put through the standards converter, then passed on to the Euro-vision network for 500 million people in Europe, all in less than a second.

The BBC converter, which is also used to change signals sent to America live or on tape from the British standard to the American, works by storing the signals relating to each line of the picture and releasing them at the right moment to take their place in a reconstituted picture at the new standard. The delay is achieved by directing the signal through quartz crystal blocks.

BBC converters have been used by both the BBC and ITN, which handles lines conversion for the ITV network, but in 1972 IBA engineers produced DICE (for Digital Intercontinental Conversion Equipment), the first fully digital (or computer-type) converter, which was claimed to be smaller and requiring less adjustment.

Television in action

Today's television picture signal may be originated in a number of ways – from live cameras in a studio or at an outside broadcast location, from film on telecine machines, from slides by means of slide scanners, from tape on a VTR machine and sometimes from a mixture of them.

Above the studio in a soundproofed control suite sits the director of the programme. Before him are monitor screens showing the picture being transmitted and the pictures available for his selection from the other cameras. On his left is his production assistant (PA) who times the programme and passes on his instructions. On his right is the vision mixer, switching between cameras on instructions, cutting by the use of a button or mixing (fading from one picture to another) by a lever.

Microphones in front of the director enable him to talk to the floor manager, his aide on the studio floor who cues the artists, and to the cameramen through headphones known as 'cans'. Behind the director or to the side of him are the lighting directors and operators, the telecine operator with filmed inserts or titles ready to roll and the 'grams' operator ready to bring in pre-recorded incidental music and sound effects.

From the studio the output goes to a master control room elsewhere, and is then routed by video and sound telecommunications circuits booked from the Post Office to other regions and the transmitters, travelling over thousands of miles of special broadband co-axial cables and microwave radio links. At the transmitters the signals are monitored, amplified and fed to aerials as high as possible on masts and towers, sometimes over 1,000 feet tall, for radiation to receivers in the area. These transmitters are mostly unattended and are either automatic or remote-controlled, serviced by flying squads of troubleshooting maintenance engineers carrying £20,000 worth of test equipment in their estate cars, but the failure rate averages only a two-minute break in 150 hours of television.

Chapter 3
Organisation

To the viewer the most obvious difference between ITV and BBC is that ITV carries advertising and the BBC channels do not. Most, though not all, viewers are aware that the BBC gets nearly all of its income from Parliamentary grants representing the licence fees paid by television owners or renters, while ITV is self-supporting, relying on money from advertisers. But there is a more important difference in the structure of the two organisations. The BBC is a giant, centrally based concern with a total staff of 26,000. It has regional offices and studios, but the centre of power and policy making is in London and the majority of programmes are made there. ITV is a federation of fifteen autonomous companies in fourteen different regions (see page 127), providing the programmes under contract with the Independent Broadcasting Authority.

The differences between the two organisations stem from their roots. The BBC is a corporation established by Royal Charter in 1927 (when it succeeded the original British Broadcasting Company) and operating under a licence from the Home Secretary, whose functions have included since 1974 the allocation of wavelengths. The charter, which grants the BBC permission to broadcast and carry on certain other activities such as publishing, was last renewed in 1964 for twelve years, but was extended in 1974 to end in July 1979.

The Independent Television Authority, which became the Independent Broadcasting Authority in 1972 when it assumed responsibility for independent local radio as well as television, was set up by the Television Act of 1954, which charged it 'to provide television services additional to those of the BBC and of high quality'. The Act also placed on the Authority the duty of seeing that programmes included nothing 'which offends against good taste or decency, or is likely to encourage or incite to crime or to lead to disorder, or to be offensive to public feeling, or which contains any offensive representation of, or reference to, a living person'.

The ban on offensive references, which would have prevented an ITV equivalent of *That Was The Week That Was*, disappeared in the Television Act of 1964, but the new Act tightened other restrictions, giving the Authority greater powers over the programme companies, including the right to ban programmes from the schedules or, equally, to insist on a programme's inclusion.

The Independent Broadcasting Authority Act of 1973 consolidated into one the Television Act and the Sound Broadcasting Act of 1972 which had given the Authority responsibility for Independent Local Radio, and an IBA Act of 1974 extended the Authority's life, like that of the BBC Charter, to 1979.

BBC structure

The BBC is presided over by a £10,000 a year chairman (since 1973 Professor Sir Michael Swann) and eleven governors appointed by the Queen in Council (which means in practice the Cabinet Office). The governors, who are not necessarily knowledgeable about television, are chosen to represent the public and are people who have distinguished themselves in a variety of fields. Appointment is usually for five years.

The governors appoint as their chief executive the Director General (since 1969 Sir Charles Curran, once a producer of talks on radio). Beneath him comes a Board of Management including managing directors and directors for Radio, Engineering, External Broadcasting, Finance and the like. The Managing Director, Television, is currently Ian Trethowan. Under him is a Director of Programmes (currently Alasdair Milne, a former editor of the *Tonight* programme), who is responsible for the policy and output of both BBC1 and 2. Each of these networks has its own controller, who decides on the programmes and schedules in conjunction with a central programmes planning department. This department allocates time slots to the heads of programme departments, who assign them to the producers who make the shows.

All planning for BBC1 and 2 is done in concert. The main television output groups produce for both networks, offering programmes for use by either network's controller, the Director of Programmes acting as a referee in maintaining a balance. There are five major production groups.

Drama. Divided into three sections, one for single plays, the second for serials like *The Brothers*, and the third for episode series like *Softly, Softly*.

Light Entertainment. Divided into two sections, one for variety like *The Morecambe and Wise Show* and the other for comedy like *It Ain't Half Hot, Mum*.

Current Affairs. Concerned with programmes like *Panorama* and *Nationwide*.

Outside Broadcasts. Divided into three sections, one for sport programmes like *Match of the Day*, a second for public occasions like Trooping the Colour and the third for shows from outside the studios, such as a concert from a theatre and *Come Dancing*.

Features. Divided into three sections, one for science programmes like *Horizon*, one for arts programmes like *Omnibus* and the third for general series like *Man Alive*.

There are also smaller departments including Documentaries, Music, Religious Programmes, Schools, Further Education and Open University, and a Presentation department responsible for programme promotion spots, announcements and weather forecasts. News is in a special category with its own chain of responsibility, the editor of the BBC's news and current affairs services reporting directly to the Director General.

Parallel to the programme groups and departments in BBC Television's operational charts come engineering, administration, personnel and finance groups, and the programme servicing departments, supervised by a Controller, Programme Services. These include the Studio Management department, the Film Operations and Services department, the Scenic Services department (which makes or provides sets and 'props'), the world's largest design group with 400 designers to work on settings, costumes, make-up, graphics and visual effects, and a Scripts Unit which sifts some 6,000 scripts sent in by hopeful writers every year, of which only about 10 per cent are of even possible interest.

ITV structure

The chairmanship of the IBA, like that of the BBC, is a £10,000 a year job, held since 1975 by Lady Plowden, an educationalist who was formerly a vice-chairman of the BBC. However, she and the ten other members of the Authority (including three with responsibilities for Scotland, Wales and Northern Ireland) are appointed by the Home Secretary instead of the Crown.

The IBA, whose staff numbers about 1,300, does not make programmes. It has four functions: to appoint the companies that provide the programmes; to control the programme output, seeing that each company provides a balance of information, education and entertainment; to control the quality and standards of the advertising; and to transmit the programmes (the IBA builds, owns and operates the ITV transmitters).

Chief executive of the IBA is the Director General; since 1970 Brian Young, a former headmaster. His headquarters staff are in eight main divisions, Programme Services, Advertising Control, Engineering, Radio, Finance (Internal and External), Information and Administrative Services.

The Programme Services division plans schedules with the companies and has the responsibility for ensuring that programmes conform with the requirements of the IBA Act. It monitors them for quality, taste, decency, political impartiality and the proportions of home-made and foreign material. Advertising Control supervises the commercials. Engineering develops and maintains the transmitting system. The Internal Finance Division pays salaries and bills incurred by the Authority; External Finance assesses and collects the government's levy on programme companies' profits.

The programmes are provided by fifteen companies in fourteen regions, London having two companies, one for weekdays and the other for weekends. One of the reasons for this is that a single company in the capital would be too rich and powerful. Independent Television News, which provides bulletins for all the companies, is a non-profit making company owned jointly by the fifteen. Combined staffs of the programme companies total nearly 11,000.

In practice, a small number of big companies in the most populated regions (often known as 'the majors' but now officially called 'central' companies) provide most of the programmes networked throughout the country; the others ('the regionals') concentrate chiefly on programmes reflecting aspects of local life for screening in their own areas, although some of their programmes are widely networked.

Before 1968 the major networking companies were four in number. They and their bases were:

Rediffusion: London weekdays.
ATV Network: the Midlands on weekdays and London at weekends.
ABC Television: the Midlands and North at weekends.
Granada Television: the North on weekdays.

But since then, due to a substantial reorganisation by the Authority, ITV has had a Big Five, which are:

Thames Television (the product of a merger between ABC and Rediffusion): London weekdays until 7 p.m. Friday.
London Weekend Television (a new company in 1968): London from 7 p.m. Friday to closedown on Sunday.
Yorkshire Television (another new company in 1968, when the former North region was split into two): Yorkshire throughout the week.
Granada Television: Lancashire throughout the week.
ATV Network: the Midlands throughout the week.

The first two are based in London; Yorkshire in Leeds; Granada in Manchester; and ATV in Birmingham.

Each of these companies has its own board and its own controller of programmes and each has the kind of programme departments that the BBC has, such as drama, light entertainment, outside broadcasts and current affairs. Each has more than 1,000 staff. Obviously this system involves a multiplication of departments and executives, but the IBA feels that it is democratically right and that it is important to diversify control of the media. The plural system is seen as providing the competition required by the Television Acts and as helping to generate ideas and programmes and opportunities for utilising them.

The ten basically regional companies, which are dealt with in detail in Chapter 14 under Regional Programmes, have fewer departments and staff but all make at least some programmes for wider showing than their own regions and some contribute regularly to the network, notably Anglia with plays and natural history and Southern with children's programmes. However, the 'regionals' supply only some 7 per cent of the networked programmes.

One department that every programme company has, but which is not found at the BBC, is a sales office to deal with the advertisers who pay for ITV.

Programme networking

Each ITV company has three sources of material open to it: programmes produced in its own studios, programmes made by other ITV companies, and programmes such as American film series which it can buy from outside sources. The Authority checks the mix for balance of programmes and acceptability of timings, seeing for instance that a fair proportion of documentaries go out before 10 p.m. and are not relegated until a late hour.

All companies produce their own basic programme schedules and these are co-ordinated, with their central core of networked programmes added, by the Programme Controllers Group which consists of the Programme Controllers of the Big Five and the IBA's Head of Programme Services with the Director of the Network Programme Secretariat in the chair. This body, which meets every week, is supplemented by the Network Programme Committee, which discusses broad policy issues and on which all the companies are represented.

Each of the central companies accepts responsibility for producing a share of the schedule equal to its share of the Big Five's combined advertising revenue. Costs of the programmes are allocated in a similar way, a company making a series adding together its actual costs plus a percentage for overheads and then dividing the total between the companies according to their percentages of the combined advertising revenue. The regional companies pay for programmes on a scale approved by the Authority.

When it comes to fixing slots for programmes, some are virtually inviolable, either by order of the IBA or by custom. The IBA rules that every company must take the news from ITN and certain current affairs programmes, that they must all show two plays a week, an arts or science programme every weekend and at least thirty-nine documentaries a year. Custom dictates that Granada has the 7.30 p.m. slot on Mondays and Wednesdays, for its *Coronation Street* has been networked then for many years. Other slots are equally reserved, but the rest involve negotiation, one company agreeing to take a programme from another in return for a reciprocal deal over a forthcoming series of its own.

Each company has its individual problems and requirements. One company may find that it is losing its audience to the BBC at a certain time and will wish to amend its schedules to provide what it regards as stronger opposition. Another may find that a programme which is popular in other areas of the country sends its own viewers early to bed. But the IBA has the last word.

Finance

Most of the BBC's income is derived from licence fees, which at the time of writing are £8 for a monochrome set and £18 for a colour set. After the Post Office, which issues the licences and investigates complaints about interference, had taken a £16 million cut for its work, the BBC received more than £146 million from this source in 1974–5. It made another £1·1 million from the sale of programmes to other countries. This and other income has, of course, to cover both television and radio; its operating and capital expenditure on television was nearly £109 million in 1974–5.

The IBA's income is mainly from rentals paid by the programme companies for the use of the Authority's transmitters and this was some £14 million in 1974–5. It spent £8·5 million of this on engineering.

The programme companies' money comes 98 per cent from the sale of advertising time (some £160 million gross in 1975) plus money from publications and the sale of programmes abroad. But the programme companies have to pay not only ordinary taxes, but also a special levy on income above a certain level, which was first imposed by the Exchequer in 1964. By 1974, though the sliding rates had varied over the years, it had exacted £217 million in all.

The companies had protested, not just at the rates but at the imposition of the levy on advertising revenue rather than on profits, and in 1974 the Chancellor heeded them and switched the levy to profits, giving the companies some incentive to increase their spending on programmes.

Advisory committees

Both the BBC and IBA have a number of advisory committees, the chief being their General Advisory Councils composed of representatives of the public with a variety of backgrounds. These committees have wide-ranging terms of reference and make recommendations about policy and programmes. They are unpaid for this work.

Both the BBC and IBA also have a number of regional committees and specialist committees on such subjects as religious and educational broadcasting and the allocation of charity appeals.

The BBC, which has fifty-two committees in all, also has specialist advisers on programmes for immigrants, on music, science, engineering and agriculture. The IBA has specialist committees on advertising. Since 1971 both bodies have also had boards to deal with complaints from organisations and individuals who believe they have been unfairly treated in television programmes.

Chapter 4

News

By the second half of the sixties surveys carried out for the ITA showed that most people in Britain claimed television as their chief source of information about what was going on in the world. ITN's main programme, *News at Ten*, was regularly in the Top Twenty and seen by twelve to fifteen million people nightly.

Yet television news as viewers know it today began in Britain only in 1955 when ITV opened in London and Independent Television News was established. The pre-war BBC Television service showed cinema newsreels from Gaumont-British and British Movietone, and for the first eight years of post-war television there were still only newsreels, though the BBC had begun making its own.

From weekly editions (with repeats) they became bi-weekly and eventually nightly, but by comparison with today's news bulletins they were leisurely and insular. A BBC publication of 1950 said they ranged 'from the week's sport to scenes at a dock strike; from the Open Air Theatre at Regent's Park to the tractors harvesting the season's wheat', and added, 'Occasionally the cameras extend their range to international happenings.'*

In 1954, with ITV on its way, the BBC introduced *Television News and Newsreel*, a nightly ten minutes consisting of a reading of the latest radio news, followed by the familiar newsreel. An unseen Richard Baker introduced the first of these programmes at 7.30 p.m. on 5 July with the words: 'Here is an illustrated summary of the news. It will be followed by the latest film of events and happenings at home and abroad.' Then the voices of John Snagge and Andrew Timothy took over, reading reports on truce talks in Indo-China, the price of meat after the ending of rationing, the Petrov spy case and tests of the Comet airliner. The illustrations were 'still' photographs and captions and the film that followed – showing a conference of doctors – was silent with an accompaniment of background music. The programme was largely illustrated radio, for the BBC still thought primarily of radio as the medium for news. Their newsreaders had been chosen for their voices rather than their visual appeal, and there was no competition to bring greater urgency to the processing and screening of film.

In fact, there was no public demand for a more visual approach and journalists who commented on the new service considered that television news could never be a practical proposition because cameramen

* *Television Story* by Frank Tilsley.

could never be sufficiently numerous, mobile or prescient to be on the spot when stories broke.

Aidan Crawley, who launched ITN, and Geoffrey Cox who took over from him as editor half way through its first year, proved them wrong. 'I had worked in America and seen the way news was handled on television there,' Crawley told me. He borrowed from America. Before the new service opened he let it be known that ITN would not have news*readers* but news*casters*. They would be chosen for their personality and would be human and friendly, compared to the aloofly formal BBC men, and would be encouraged to rewrite turgid official statements to suit their own styles. Unlike their American counterparts they would also go out of the studio on reporting assignments.

Many of the public had misgivings, for the word 'newscaster' suggested a show-biz American approach, but at 10 p.m. on 22 September 1955, ITV's opening night, the first of the new-style newscasts was presented by a twenty-four-year-old named Christopher Chataway, who was already known to the public as a record-breaking runner. The *Daily Telegraph* reported next morning,

> Chris Chataway made a courageous and partly successful effort to improve upon the BBC. He spoke confidently and naturally, though he looked a little worried and once cast a glimpse sideways as if he were trying to look over his shoulder at some track competitor. He included the un-BBC-like item of a brief account of the Jack Spot trial. [Jack Spot was a notorious gangster, a self-proclaimed boss of London's underworld.] Film illustrations in this bulletin were also more profuse and effective than those usually seen in BBC bulletins.

Crime was an area to which ITN gave more coverage than the BBC had ever done. They also included unimportant but amusing 'human stories' about ordinary people, which had long been a feature of popular newspapers but had seldom found a place in the BBC bulletins. On Crawley's instructions, ITN reporters were not deferential when interviewing statesmen but began the policy, which is accepted generally today, of treating them as men from whom straight answers could be sought. Under Geoffrey Cox, who came to television from Fleet Street, ITN pursued scoops and exclusives with an avidity new to British broadcasting. When Robin Day scooped the world by interviewing President Nasser in Cairo at a time when Britain, in the aftermath of Suez, had no diplomatic links at all with Egypt, television was showing itself a real pacemaker in news coverage. Above all it sought, by thrusting its cameras into the face of the news, to exploit television's unique strength – to let the public see news – or a great deal of news – as it happened.

Where the BBC had seemed as much a part of the establishment as *The Times* was then, ITN set out to woo viewers by the sort of methods that the *Daily Mirror* used to attract readers.

Chataway and his fellow newscasters, including the bespectacled, bow-tied young barrister, Robin Day, and a dark-haired Old Etonian writer named Ludovic Kennedy, soon had the same sort of popular following known until then only by TV panellists. The BBC, which had already begun showing its newsreaders on the screen, soon followed ITN's style, and its team of Robert Dougall, Kenneth Kendall and Richard Baker also became household names.

The BBC also developed its film coverage quickly, engaging in a competitive battle which resulted in the rapid development of television into the main source of news for the British public.

Over the years the two services have moved to middle ground, ITN less brash, the BBC more human, and both have won the respect of Press and public alike.

Today's news programmes

BBC Television News is a part of the BBC's over-all news and current affairs organisation. ITN is a non-profit making subsidiary of the ITV programme companies, and is owned jointly by them. It costs them nearly £5 million a year, though since *News at Ten* commands big audiences, the advertising rates for commercials screened before, during and after it are commensurately high and the companies get a good return.

Total staff of ITN is about 460, of which 100 are journalists. BBC TV News has a smaller budget but about 500 employees and can also call on the staff and facilities of radio news.

ITN puts out three bulletins every weekday: the lunch-time *First Report*, the 5.50 p.m. *News* (known at ITN as 'the early') and *News at Ten* (known as 'the late'). The pattern is similar on BBC1 and both networks show late night regional news. BBC2 puts out two bulletins on weekdays. There are also, of course, special bulletins giving live coverage of major events like moon shots and the Budget.

Newest of the regular programmes are the lunch-time ones, which followed the lifting of governmental restrictions on hours of broadcasting in 1972. At ITN, Robert Kee, a veteran of current affairs programmes, was brought in to present *First Report* as virtually a one-man show in which he announced, the news, conducted studio interviews and even read letters from viewers. He was succeeded by Leonard Parkin in 1976.

Chief programmes on the two main channels are the late evening shows: the *Nine O'Clock News* on BBC1 and *News at Ten* on ITN. It was ITN that pioneered regular half-hour news bulletins at peak time

Early days of News at Ten – *Alastair Burnet and Reginald Bosanquet*

when it introduced *News at Ten* in 1967. This was a gamble that many felt would fail, as it was widely believed then that a half hour of news would be more than the public would accept. Cox – who had been knighted the previous year – had argued for this development for years, but even he found his faith tested at the start of the experiment.

Sir Geoffrey recalls:

The first three nights were a mess. We were so anxious to do something new, so anxious to avoid the charge that we were just making a longer version of the old 9 p.m. news that we were committing the worst of all sins of the newsman – we drifted away from telling the news. We had got so accustomed to cutting down and cramming even big stories into two or three minutes that we did not believe the viewer would take them at greater length, so we were filling the latter part of the programme with feature stories or studio discussions.

By the third day I knew we had lost our way so I told our morning planning conference, 'Let us stop experimenting and go back to what we know we can do – simply make a longer version of the old 9 p.m. news.'

That night we received from Alan Hart and our camera crew in Aden one of the most vivid film news stories television has ever presented – the Argyll and Sutherland Highlanders seizing the Crater district of Aden back from the rebels. It had action, tension, danger – and a television natural in Colonel Mitchell. We ran it for 11 minutes – virtually the length of the old 9 p.m. bulletin. It held the viewer for every second. From then on we had a formula which worked – play each story as hard as the news in it permitted. When the viewing figures came in at the end of the week we knew we had the viewers with us.*

With *News at Ten* in the Top Twenty programmes, the BBC was forced to extend the news on its main channel as well, moving it forward to 9 p.m. Later it also adopted the *News at Ten* system of two newscasters, begun in 1967 by Alastair Burnet and Andrew Gardner. Incidentally, the reason for having two newscasters – another practice already in use in America – is not merely a desire to ensure that the viewer will not grow bored with one man: it has the practical advantage that, with news continuing to come in while the programme is on the air, fresh briefings can be given to whichever newscaster is out of camera shot. However, in 1976, the BBC reverted to the use of a single news reader.

Getting the news to the screen

Newscasters are, of course, the TV newsmen best known to viewers. They come from a variety of backgrounds. Peter Woods of the BBC is a veteran of Fleet Street reporting while Richard Baker was briefly a teacher and an actor before becoming a radio announcer. ITN's Reginald Bosanquet joined ITN fresh from university as a sub-editor before ITV went on the air, while Andrew Gardner was a radio reporter.

Newscasters of the future are most likely to arrive in the job from work as television reporters, starting perhaps in one of the regions. The job has specialised techniques, such as learning to put questions so that they produce more than 'yes' or 'no' answers, and getting to the heart of a story with the fewest possible questions.

Television reporters travel the world, covering perhaps a rail accident at home one day and a famine in Africa the next. The job can be dangerous. Covering the Biafran war in 1968, ITN reporter Peter Sissons was on his way to the front with a cameraman, a sound recordist, other newsmen and a handful of Federal troops when their Land Rovers were halted by a trench dug in the road. So they got out and walked – into an ambush. Sissons began commentating into his microphone, then tried to crawl towards a depression in the ground, but he came into the sights of a sniper only twenty-five yards away and took a bullet in each leg. After the rebels had been driven off he was wheeled back to the Land Rover in an old pram found by the roadside before being driven to Port Harcourt for blood transfusions. Viewers saw the whole event on television. Sissons subsequently

* *TV Times*, 1 July 1971.

ITN cameraman and sound recordist await action

became ITN's Industrial Editor but some newsmen have not returned from covering wars.

A reporter generally works with a 'crew' consisting of a film cameraman and a sound recordist; sometimes also a lighting engineer where interior shots are required. ITN has sixteen such crews (and can also call on crews from the regional ITV companies). The BBC has twenty-five crews. However, a cameraman will sometimes be sent alone on a story that does not justify the attendance of a reporter and sound recordist. A commentary will be written later by a scriptwriter in the studio, working from news agency reports and the 'dope sheet' of caption material that the cameraman sends in with his film, often by a despatch rider equipped with a powerful motorcycle to rush film to the laboratories.

The news organisations also employ electronic television cameras for live transmissions, perhaps to cover the announcement of a by-election result, which normally is now known to viewers at home even before it is announced to the crowds waiting outside the town hall. These cameras are carried in outside broadcast vans that are also equipped with video-recording machines and facilities for two-way conversations between presenter in the studio and reporter in the remote location.

Reporters and crews are the outside men of the TV news organisations, but there are many more in the background in the offices – producers who are in charge of particular bulletins, directors who supervise the studio work, copytasters who assess the potential of stories coming in from news and film agencies and scriptwriters who prepare commentaries to films and leads in and out for the newscasters. (Writing for news bulletins is different from writing for a newspaper, for the words must be capable of being spoken easily; at the BBC copy is usually dictated to typists to ensure that the words read well.)

There are sub-editors to cut stories to length, to check and polish them, and librarians who can produce film or still pictures from their files. And incidentally, like newspapers, they maintain obituaries (but their 'obits' are on film) of prominent people, which are updated regularly for instant use when required. There are graphics departments to prepare maps, diagrams and charts against the clock and props departments that can build models of, say, spacecraft. Long shifts of twelve and fourteen hours for several days at a time are common in order to preserve continuity.

On a typical day at the ITN headquarters not far from Oxford Street the editorial floor begins to come alive at 8 a.m. The duty news editor, having already digested the contents of the morning papers and listened to the latest radio bulletin in search of stories to be followed up, talks to news editors of the regional ITV companies to see what they have in prospect. He then begins up-dating the schedule for the day. (Some reporters and crews will already have been despatched to cover events listed in the diary.)

The foreign news editor is performing a similar task, assessing what can be expected from ITN staff abroad, from UPITN (a news agency in which ITN is a partner and which has its own staff in foreign capitals), and from the news organisations of television companies in other countries.

At 10.30 editor Nigel Ryan holds his daily conference attended by the producers of the three bulletins, the duty news and foreign editors, the assignments editor in charge of film crews, the chief sub-editors and other executives. The conference ranges over the schedules and lasts about twenty minutes, after which there are reporters and camera crews to be briefed.

The editorial floor fills up. There are three main desks, one for each of the programmes, each manned by a producer, chief sub-editor, copytaster, director and newscaster. Some stories may run through all three bulletins, but they will be updated as the day goes on and *News at Ten* has time for more detailed coverage.

At midday the producers of 'the early' and 'the late' programmes hold conferences at their desks while the *First Report* team move into the studio on the floor below. *First Report* goes out and attention is concentrated on 'the early'. Reporters and cameramen are leaving and returning, the telephones are in constant use, agency tape machines are punching out the same news reports that are going into newspaper offices. 'The early' goes and all efforts are bent to the big programme.

At 7 p.m., after an early supper break, the producer holds a final conference. The running order is rearranged. The biggest story must come first, whether or not there is film. Second place can be justified for a story that is good visually. Another story may have to come late in the running order because of the time element – a reporter may be kicking his heels at Heathrow awaiting the arrival of a politician who should have something to tell.

Graphics produce diagrams and maps, News Information produce still pictures, scriptwriters co-ordinate copy, linking it to the film that is being edited in five cutting rooms flanking the main room. Sub-editors prune copy to bring down the running length.

At 8 p.m. a technical rehearsal begins in the studio. There are four cameras, two for the newscasters and two for captions, pictures and studio discussions. Typists tap out stories and links on narrow rolls that are fitted to the teleprompters. The newscasters will read the words from a monitor screen below the camera lens, though they will also have typed scripts in front of them.

At 9.30 newscasters and editorial staff move to the studio for re-hearsal. The newscasters alter a word or two, underline a difficult name. The programme is over-long, but that is deliberate: it will be pruned to its exact twenty-six minutes and thirty seconds on transmission.

In the control room the director and his assistants sit before a battery of monitor screens showing the shot on camera and other shots available. Film and tape are ready on the telecine and videotape machines. The director's PA begins her countdown. 'Five . . . four . . . three . . .'. Big Ben begins to boom and a newscaster begins to inter-polate the headlines – 'the bongs' as they are known at ITN. The director calls the shots to the vision mixer sitting in front of a three-foot-wide bank of panel buttons. The programme cuts smoothly from the newscaster to film and tape from all parts of the world, to captions and maps, to a live report from a provincial city, to more film and back to the newscaster.

The half-way break gives two minutes for checking on the state of the second half and then it is back into the programme. When it is over the director calls the traditional, 'Thank you, studio', and the staff drift away, discussing the programme. A sub-editor stays late at his desk to watch for a major story breaking, for ITN never closes. If something happens a flash will be prepared for companies to cut into the programme being screened.

Watching the monitor screens in ITN's control room

World-wide coverage

The biggest change in the news programmes since 1955 has been in the speed of communications. Film rather than tape remains the chief ingredient of news programmes because it is still quicker and more economical to despatch a film crew rather than an outside broadcast unit, though this may well change before long. Today the cameraman shoots colour film, yet the laboratories can process it within thirty minutes so that film received as *News at Ten* begins can be included before the programme ends.

Jet travel has shrunk the world so that staff can get quickly to most parts of it and – just as important – get film back fast. ITN now maintains only one permanently based foreign correspondent – in Washington – though it has 'stringers' (non-staff cameramen and reporters operating on a freelance basis) everywhere. But there are now quicker ways of getting pictures across the world than by flying cans of film into London.

There are normally three daily exchanges of news film by land-line links between the member organisations of the European Broadcasting Union, which include the television news companies of Europe and Scandinavia, plus Morocco, Algeria and Tunisia and also Turkey, Jordan and Israel. Film of a football match in Holland will be offered by Netherlands Television to other members; ITN and the

BBC, who are both members, may offer film of a royal occasion or a bomb explosion in London. Every morning the foreign editors confer over the telephone about the stories that are being covered or will be covered during the day. Then they telex the EBU's Geneva headquarters requisitions for the stories they want to take, and the technical headquarters in Brussels organise the circuits and lines necessary.

The first exchange, known as EVN (for Eurovision) Zero is at noon; the main exchange – EVN1 – is at 5 p.m. and EVN2 is at 7.30 p.m. There are also 'flash' offers of urgent film, such as an assassination attempt, and 'specials' on events of international interest. The material is screened on closed-circuit and countries that want it tape it. No fees change hands. Every country takes out at some time, but every country also puts in. The only costs are the operational expenses, towards which all the companies pay their share.

Iron Curtain countries have a similar co-operative organisation to the EBU, known as OIRT, and hold similar exchanges. Austrian television monitors OIRT for the EBU with the sanction of the Iron Curtain countries, who reciprocally tape some material (though not as much) from Eurovision.

Film or live coverage from farther-off countries can be transmitted by a communications earth satellite. Four main satellites linking the world are owned by Intelsat in which seventy-six countries participate. Satellite transmissions are now routine, though not everyday occurrences, for they can be costly, particularly if a company books a 'gateway' for an exclusive transmission from America, but if the story is of interest to most European countries (as were the Watergate investigations) costs can be shared between companies.

The funeral of President Kennedy was seen in Britain as it happened, relayed from Washington by satellite. Viewers in Britain were able to see an Apollo capsule heading for its splashdown before even the crew of the recovery carrier on the spot – due to a television camera in a helicopter.

Most satellite transmissions to Britain are from America, but they have also come from Japan, Australia, Hong Kong, Bangkok and Manila, and Jordan and Israel which are linked to the EBU by satellite.

British television news teams sometimes combine the use of aircraft, satellites and land lines. For example, during the war in Cyprus in 1974, film shot by British cameramen was flown to Tel Aviv where it was processed, then satellited to Rome, where it was fed into the Eurovision network and transmitted to London.

The television news organisations can now get pictures back to London from any part of the world – fast.

Chapter 5

Documentaries and current affairs

In newspaper terms the current affairs and documentary programmes of television constitute the main feature pages. Any factual programme longer than a news item may be classed as a documentary, but current affairs programmes are concerned with the topical and immediate, enlarging on, or supplying background to, the news of the day, week or month. Almost inevitably they involve controversy and often problems of political balance. Documentaries on the other hand are not necessarily topical. They may deal with the Second World War or holidays abroad or prison reform; they may be the personalised reportage of Alan Whicker or Trevor Philpott. But they may still be controversial, particularly when dealing with social issues such as homelessness or poverty.

This area of television journalism has evolved its own stars. For example, Robin Day, unrivalled at the high-level political interview; James Cameron, master of the written commentary; Alastair Burnet, unequalled as an ad-libbing anchor man for running programmes such as the coverage of a general election.

The BBC may have moved cautiously into the field of daily television news, but it showed imagination and daring in current affairs and news-in-depth programmes. The motivation came largely from one producer, Grace Wyndham Goldie, who envisaged at an early stage what television might achieve in this field and gathered around her a team of young and enterprising producers including Donald Baverstock, Michael Peacock and Huw Wheldon.

Today's current affairs series

Oldest of the current affairs series still screened is *Panorama*, which began in 1953 as a fortnightly general purpose magazine subtitled 'a reflection on the contemporary scene'. It was received without marked enthusiasm until the arrival of Malcolm Muggeridge as an interviewer of the famous.

In 1955, as ITV began, *Panorama* was relaunched as a peak-time weekly programme to concentrate on important subjects. Richard Dimbleby, television's supreme commentator on national events, was brought in to add his authority as link man, and the programme achieved the greatest prestige in television. Cabinet ministers and MPs

Richard Dimbleby introducing Panorama

came to the studio when bidden. When a rail strike was threatened in 1962 Dimbleby brought about a televised confrontation between the Minister of Transport and the General Secretary of the National Union of Railwaymen before they had begun official meetings and was accused of trying to usurp the role of the Minister of Labour. It was one of the earliest complaints of this kind.

Panorama had other scoops, such as interviewing Georges Bidault, the exiled French politician, in London at a time when the Home Office was denying that he was in the country. It was flexible, sometimes using its full fifty minutes on one subject and sometimes including three or four items.

It established the classic current affairs format of a film report followed by a studio debate and was not deterred from tackling an important subject by the fact that it might make dull viewing; but it could unbend on occasion. In 1957 Dimbleby hoaxed the country with an April Fool item on spaghetti trees, which caused such a sensation that a spaghetti tree created by the BBC design department had pride of place at the programme's twentieth anniversary party in 1973.

Panorama and Dimbleby were so closely identified that his death in 1965 was a major blow to the programme. Dimbleby was one of the first victims of cancer to make the nature of his illness known, which he did because, he said, he was 'strongly opposed to the idea of cancer being an unmentionable disease'. At a memorial service in Westminster Abbey, which Dimbleby had helped to make familiar to millions through his commentaries, the former Archbishop of Canterbury, Lord Fisher, said: 'Richard Dimbleby established a new art and a new profession of communicating to the people by a commentary the outward form and the inward meaning of great occasions, both in Church and State.'

The Dimbleby name has continued in current affairs. David Dimbleby, his elder son, took his father's old chair in the *Panorama* studio in 1966 to introduce a special edition on cancer, went on to establish himself in such programmes as *The Dimbleby Talk-in*, and in 1974, on the 21st birthday of *Panorama*, became resident link man on the programme. Meanwhile, his brother Jonathan had joined ITV's *This Week* and in 1974 won an award named after their father for the previous year's most important contribution to factual television, a programme on famine in Ethiopia.

Thames Television's *This Week* is ITV's longest running current affairs series, though its programmes are only of thirty minutes compared to *Panorama*'s fifty. When it began in 1956 the thirty minutes were crowded with an average of six contrasting items a week. Items ranged from polygamy to black magic and from Sir Bernard Docker, the financier, to Alfred Hinds, the escaper. Brian Connell was chief anchor man until 1963 after which it was left to each reporter to introduce his own story.

This Week now covers only one story in each issue, largely because of the increased length of the news bulletins, which frequently devote six or seven minutes to a single item; this has resulted in deeper coverage of stories by the current affairs series. Its greatest rival is not the BBC's *Panorama* but another ITV series, *World in Action*.

Granada's *World in Action* brought a new style to current affairs when it arrived on the screen without any advance publicity in January 1963. Its first chief was Tim Hewat, a forceful, restless, Australian journalist who had earlier produced *Searchlight*, a Northern regional series. There was no link man. No reporter was seen and the commentary was limited to a voice over. There was no studio discussion. *World in Action* was visual. People talking were sound radio, said Hewat. His programme policy was one of profiles and exposés.

His first programme was on the atomic arms race and had actors playing Kennedy and Khrushchev scowling at each other through a forest of missiles. In a subsequent programme cameras were installed in a cupboard fitted with a one-way mirror to film industrial spies planting bugging equipment. When typhoid broke out in Zermatt at the height of the Swiss winter sports season Hewat arrived with a camera crew and a hastily purchased stock of twenty-seven bottles of wine and sixty bars of chocolate to avoid possible danger from local food and water. For this he was pelted with rocks by the Swiss locals who were not keen on publicity about the outbreak.

When a group of Egyptians kidnapped an alleged Israeli spy in Rome, drugged him and strapped him in a specially fitted trunk for freighting to the Middle East, *World in Action* went to Rome and reconstructed the incident. They made a replica of the trunk in their hotel basement and, by buying a truck for £500 and painting it with the insignia of the United Arab airline, were able to drive it on to the airport tarmac where amateur actors playing Arab diplomats unloaded it while the cameras turned.

Hewat later left ITV for Australia but the programme found equally tough successors. *World in Action* men have posed as arms dealers in Geneva and hippo hunters in Rhodesia. They have had a cameraman shot in Jordan, a producer beaten up in Uganda and a reporter jailed in Austria. They have also had programmes banned by the ITA, notably one that Hewat made about Britain's defence expenditure in which one shot showed money pouring down a drain. The ITA was thought to have banned it for lack of balance because it did not include a government spokesman justifying the expenditure.

London Weekend Television's *Weekend World*, introduced in 1972 after the de-restriction of hours, returned to the formula of a chairman (Peter Jay, economics editor of *The Times* and son of Labour MP Douglas Jay) and to a range of items. It pleased the IBA who called it 'the most ambitious and significant current affairs development on ITV since the introduction of *News at Ten* . . . a weekly counterpart of the responsible Sunday Press',* but only a relatively small audience appeared to be available at lunchtime on Sunday.

Landmarks in current affairs

Of the current affairs series that no longer exist the most mourned has been the BBC's original *Tonight*. It began in 1957 when the so-called 'toddlers' truce' – the closed period between 6 and 7 p.m. – ended. Donald Baverstock, a Welsh ex-schoolteacher, was given forty minutes of this time five nights a week for *Tonight*, which was based on a series called *Highlight*, which he had introduced in 1955 when a newspaper strike had closed Fleet Street for a fortnight and the BBC had offered air time to journalists whose work could not be published.

Tonight fought with *Panorama* for cabinet ministers and *Monitor* (a Sunday night magazine programme introduced in 1958) for artists, but its main material consisted of stories from its roving reporters. Fyfe Robertson, Trevor Philpott and others came to it after the collapse of

* IBA Annual Report, 1973.

the magazine *Picture Post* in 1957, and Alan Whicker joined from the Exchange Telegraph news agency. The programme had a light touch to fit the early evening time. It enjoyed the bizarre and the eccentric and it ended with a topical calypso. It was also very much a live programme: Cliff Michelmore, the link man, often had no idea what item he would be required to introduce next.

Tonight begat *24 Hours*, which began in 1965 and whose presenters included Michelmore and the late Kenneth Allsop. It was a late-night series but it was not given much of a chance: its starting time varied from night to night according to the length of preceding programmes and it was inclined to be a predictable examination of the main item of the day's news. It yielded to *Midweek*, on Tuesday, Wednesday and Thursday, which gave way in 1975 to a new-style *Tonight*.

The early evening slot was later occupied by *Nationwide*, with Michael Barratt and Frank Bough, incorporating regional current affairs seen in individual regions within a framework of national material. On ITV at the same viewing time, the current affairs programmes are entirely regional.

Tonight was also largely responsible for *That Was The Week That Was*, which was in 1962 the first of the BBC's satire series, for it was devised by ex-*Tonight* men like Baverstock, Anthony Jay, Alasdair Milne and Ned Sherrin. It was expected to reach a modest-sized late night audience on Saturdays but became the most talked about show on television with an audience of ten million.

Sherrin gave it a deliberately amateurish look: cameras showed other cameras, boom microphones and artists moving into position. It overran its allotted time regularly. It used a huge team of writers, among them journalists, novelists and playwrights including Peter Shaffer, John Braine, Gerald Kauffman, Quentin Crewe, Dennis Potter and Kenneth Tynan. Its front man was David Frost, virtually unknown when the series began. It had the *Tonight* calypso feature (sung by Lance Percival) and also a song based on the news of the week sung by Millicent Martin. The actors in sketches included Roy Kinnear, Kenneth Cope and Eleanor Bron, and there was cartoonist Timothy Birdsall who was to die tragically young from leukaemia.

Through *Not So Much a Programme, More a Way of Life* in 1964 it grew to three nights a week. Much of it was comedy material belonging to the light entertainment sector, but much of it commented on current affairs and it could be cruel. No one and nothing was sacrosanct. The Church, cabinet ministers and industrialists were pilloried, and the controversy was fierce. Mrs Mary Whitehouse emerged as one of the leaders of protest, and Sir Hugh Greene, the Director General, was vilified. Sunday newspapers ran the number of complaints each week like football league tables. When Bernard Levin referred to Sir Alec Douglas-Home in the programme as a cretin, Sir Hugh had to apologise.

Eventually the programme died, but its influence had been great, and it begat, among other programmes, the Frost series of interviews.

Chat shows and discussions

Starting with *Picture Page* in 1936 there had been many interview programmes on television, but in 1960 John Freeman gave them a new stature with the BBC's *Face to Face*. His programmes opened with drawings of the subject by Feliks Topolski which merged into a close-up picture of the subject, who was kept in tight close-up. Viewers saw only the back of Freeman's head. His technique was superb. Often he opened with a curious question, the significance of which became apparent only later, and he fashioned the interviews cleverly, allowing the subject to talk freely on any question, yet he was always able to steer the conversation back to a logical sequence. When he interviewed Stirling Moss, the racing driver, Freeman began with his religious beliefs and led into his feelings when driving at speeds beyond the limits of safety. His most controversial interview was with Gilbert Harding, who broke down and wept when Freeman pursued questions about his mother.

The Frost interviews began in 1966. He used a big team of researchers to track down and sign celebrities and to brief him with background material. His own gifts were in establishing easy relations with the famous and asking directly the questions that viewers wanted answered. One of the best examples was his interview with the Roman Catholic Archbishop Heenan about the Pope's encyclical on birth control and contraception.

The interviews were conducted before invited audiences, usually packed with people holding strong views on the subjects under discussion, and Frost would then bring in and 'orchestrate' the audience (as he described it to me). This led sometimes to criticism. His interviews with Emil Savundra, the financier, and John Petro, the drug addicts' doctor, caused an outcry against 'trial by television'.

Frost told me once,

> I find the live show or the 'live-on-tape' show with a guest and an audience the exciting thing. You are doing so many different things at the same time. You're talking to someone, you're thinking 'Shall I press that point or shall I move on to another? How many minutes before the next commercial? Shall I bring in and orchestrate the audience?' You're making lots of split second decisions every split second and that's terrific.

But with his ever-increasing performing and business interests in both America and Britain, with comedy shows as well as interviews, he was criticised for moving towards show business interviews in which he was simpering and sycophantic.

Most other chat-show hosts, who have included Eamonn Andrews, Michael Parkinson, Russell Harty, Derek Nimmo, Jimmy Savile and Simon Dee, always relied more on show business guests.

In the early sixties there was a vogue for after-dinner conversation programmes. In an ATV series called *Dinner Party* Lord Boothby talked to guests over the port and brandy with a camera concealed behind a partition to avoid inhibiting the talk. One financial journalist had his tongue loosened so effectively that the director had to keep the camera off him, with the result that a disembodied voice was heard from time to time trying to slur its way into the conversation while Boothby and the other guests ignored it and refused even to look in the direction of the voice.

Later this vogue was replaced by one for phone-in programmes in which a studio guest answered questions put by viewers at home. This technique was much favoured by *Midweek*.

Political controversy

Controversy is, of course, the meat of current affairs programmes, but sometimes controversy surrounds the programme itself. Politicians are touchy in their relations with television.

Few problems arose until television had grown into a national medium in the fifties. The BBC then had a programme called *In the News*, the regular panel of which consisted of two right wingers, Lord Boothby and W. J. Brown, and two left wingers, Michael Foot and A. J. P. Taylor, whose squabbles delighted many viewers. The Conservative and Labour parties objected that the speakers were not properly or officially representative of their policies and beliefs; they wanted better party men substituted, so the BBC dropped the programme, whereupon ITV took it over with the same four under the appropriate title, *Free Speech*.

Then came a row over the so-called 'Fourteen-Day Rule'. The BBC had observed for a long time an agreement with the leaders of the main parties not to anticipate Parliamentary debates by broadcasting controversial material about subjects to be discussed within the following fortnight. In 1955, the year that ITV began, the agreement was enforced on both organisations by a formal notice from the government. Television men fought it. Newspapers were free both to discuss and express their own opinions on matters of public concern. The television organisations were – and are – forbidden to editorialise, but they did not see why they should be prevented from broadcasting balanced views on subjects until after Parliament had acted, and in 1956 the fourteen-day rule was revoked.

Problems of balance still arose. The original policy was to try and observe a balance within every programme, to have equal numbers of speakers for every viewpoint and to allow them the same amount of time. But programmes became so balanced that a viewer could not reach any conclusion. It was also difficult to contrive a balance when one side might wish to reserve its return volley to a broadside from the other until a later date. Relaxation of the requirement was inevitable.

When he was Director General of the BBC Sir Hugh Greene explained the new policy in these words:

> We have to balance different points of view in our programmes but not necessarily within each individual programme. Nothing is more stultifying than the current affairs programme in which all the opposing opinions cancel each other out. In general it makes for greater liveliness and impact if the balance can be achieved over a period, perhaps within a series of related programmes.*

Problems still remain, particularly at election times, for a candidate is guilty of illegal practice under the Representation of the People Act of 1969 if he takes part in a broadcast about his constituency when a rival candidate declines to take part and objects to the broadcast being made without his participation.

A generally unloved part of television is the party political broadcast. The first agreement on these programmes was signed by the BBC in 1947. Every year a certain amount of broadcasting time is offered to the main political parties who decide on its allocation between themselves in proportion to their vote at the previous general election. Extra broadcasts are arranged in the campaigning period preceding a general election, when any party nominating 50 or more candidates on a national basis qualifies for time.

For the general election in October 1974 the Labour and Conservative parties each had five broadcasts of ten minutes' duration, the Liberals had four of ten minutes and the National Front had one of five minutes. The Scottish National Party had two of ten minutes each in Scotland only and the Welsh National Party had one of ten minutes in Wales only.

The most objectionable feature of party political broadcasts in most viewers' eyes is the fact that they are normally shown on all channels simultaneously. Viewers – grown accustomed to seeing politicians' views challenged in current affairs programmes – have sometimes protested at this exclusive use of peak-hour viewing time for the presentation of a one-sided picture and the reviling of opponents.

However, British television has still no right to cover Parliamentary proceedings, a right that in some countries is taken for granted. A

* *BBC Handbook*, 1974.

Crowds awaiting the 1970 general election results on large television screens

Edward Heath facing John Edwards for This Week

Dutch television executive said to me, 'Of course we have the right; this is a democratic country. But we only give live coverage to debates of particular interest; at other times it is too dull.'

In 1966 MPs rejected by one vote a proposal to allow experimental closed-circuit television of their proceedings. There were various objections: that the lighting would grill members on their benches (to which the companies replied that modern cameras require little extra lighting); that television would destroy the intimacy of the House (to which television men retorted that MPs were not elected to enjoy club life but to govern); that to show proceedings in the Chamber when members were busy in committee rooms would give the impression that they did not attend debates regularly (to which the reply was that no one would want to screen routine proceedings).

The television authorities were, in fact, asking for cameras and microphones to be installed at the House and the right to plug into the proceedings at any time, either to transmit them live or to record them for transmission later in an edited version. Further attempts to achieve this were defeated by twenty-six votes in 1972, twenty-five votes in 1974 and twelve votes in 1975, a free vote being allowed in each case.

Periodically a row flares up between television and politicians over alleged bias in a programme. The two live in uneasy co-existence, needing, yet suspicious of, each other. There was a major brush between television and government in January 1972 when BBC1 announced a programme entitled *The Question of Ulster – an Enquiry into the Future*. The BBC had invited Lord Devlin to chair it and representatives of various factions (though not the IRA) to take part. Home Secretary Reginald Maudling held that such a programme would be irresponsible and inflammatory but the BBC claimed the same freedom to discuss Ulster as the Press. The broadcast went out, was responsible and was widely considered to be dull.

Brian Young, Director General of the IBA, has summed up the situation in these words:

> The view of British governments has always been that television is free to criticise, to comment and to probe, provided that this is done fairly and with a real awareness of both sides of the question. It must be impartial rather than partisan, since it holds a monopoly position, but governments have always recognised that television must be free to challenge an official line as well as to support such a line. So a democracy needs broadcasting services which are not run by government and this has always been accepted. . . . Members of Parliament believe that as elected representatives their views on all matters should carry weight and so they do. But if they were al-

lowed to carry over-riding weight, then the way would be open for general political control over broadcasting.*

Documentaries

The documentary programme that has been seen by more people than any other is *Royal Family*, 105 minutes in the company of the Queen and her family, produced in 1969 by a joint ITV/BBC consortium and directed by Richard Cawston. It was watched by twenty-three million people at its premiere on BBC1 and fifteen million (six million of them seeing it for the second time) when it was shown on ITV. It has been repeated since on both channels, given two coast-to-coast showings in America and screened in a total of 112 different countries.

Some of the biggest budget programmes have been on war. They reached their climax in 1973 with *World at War*, a twenty-six-part series by Thames Television's Jeremy Isaacs which was four years in the making and cost £1 million. It had Laurence Olivier as narrator and the research was exhaustive. Apart from war film the series had fresh interviews with such personalities as Admiral Doenitz, the German U-boat commander, Marshal of the Royal Air Force Sir Arthur Harris, war-time chief of Bomber Command, film actor James Stewart, who flew Liberators, and Traudl Junge, who was Hitler's personal secretary.

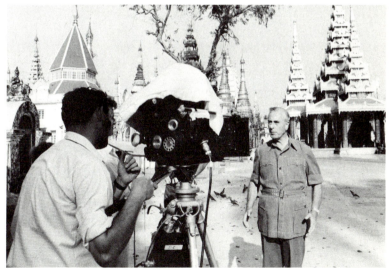

Thames Television filming in Rangoon for The Life and Times of Lord Mountbatten

* ITV 1974.

Escalating production costs caused the BBC to seek financial backing from the United States by enlisting American film and publishing companies as co-producers of series requiring large budgets, such as *America*, the 13-part history of the country seen through the eyes of Alistair Cooke. This form of backing also made possible Christopher Rallings's series, *The Search for the Nile* and *The Fight Against Slavery* and the practice spread to include major drama series and was adopted by some ITV companies.

Adrian Cowell is an independent producer who has specialised in far off locales. His *Tribe That Hides from Man* and *The Opium Warlords*, both shown by ITV, were filmed in the Amazon jungle of Brazil and the Shan States of Burma respectively. Yet it is not necessary to go far in search of subjects. A memorable documentary of 1973 was *Too Long a Winter*, Barry Cockcroft's programme for Yorkshire Television about Hannah Hauxwell, farming 200 acres in the Pennines single-handed from a dilapidated house with no running water or electricity. Letters poured in praising the programme and its heroine, in whom viewers found a serene beauty despite her white hair and tattered clothes.

And although Alan Whicker has travelled the world, immaculately groomed and mockingly alert for the offbeat from millionaires and their wives and such incredible characters as 'Papa Doc' Duvalier, the late President of Haiti, one of his best remembered programmes was

Alan Whicker visits a convent of 'Poor Clares'

an interview with wealthy Percy Shaw, the man who invented cats' eyes studs for the roads, whom Whicker found living in a house sparsely furnished apart from a number of television sets.

The scope of documentary programmes is wide, from series like *Man Alive*, with its insights into human situations such as divorce and single parenthood, to *The Money Programme* and financial situations. From *On the Braden Beat* which, apart from its comedy element, was a pioneer in consumer affairs, to *Europa*, showing the viewpoint of television programmes in other countries.

The newest trend in TV journalism as the seventies began was open access television, based on experiments in America, in which programme time was made available to outsiders to put forward their points of view. One of the first such programmes was on HTV. Then in 1973 the BBC set up a Community Programmes Unit and introduced *Open Door*. Any group wanting to put across a message on BBC2 was able to ask for forty minutes' air time.

There was no political or moral censorship, and hippies and nudists were as eligible as Scouts or moral reformers. The main stipulation was that programmes must have a national rather than local application. Within a short time the BBC had 328 applications, enough to keep the series going for six years. Early programmes were on the Gypsy council, urinary infection and the admission of women to the clergy. But the format seemed even better suited to regional television, judging by experiments by Tyne Tees Television which provided a platform for such local organisations as the Durham Cyrenians (offering help for the homeless), the Hartlepool Ratepayers' Action Group and the Teesside Consumer Group.

Chapter 6

Sport

The British are, of course, sport mad, as everyone with no enthusiasm for it has observed from time to time. And nowhere in television is rivalry as keen as it is between the sports departments of the BBC and ITV. The BBC is the keener, putting out more than 1,100 hours of sport a year (673 of them on BBC1) averaging some 13 per cent of its air time, second only to the time devoted to current affairs, documentaries and features together, and more than is given to light entertainment or drama.*

ITV viewers are offered half that amount, including thirty-four hours of wrestling. However, ITV's production is considerably higher than this, because much of its sport, including football matches and news reports, is regionalised.

Sport can win huge audiences. Normally, football commands the biggest: a Cup Final may be watched by twenty-four million people, though a big fight such as the 1971 contest between Muhammad Ali and Joe Frazier is as big a draw. Yet, in the early days of television, sport was small time. Live football was virtually non-existent and boxing meant chiefly amateurs. Major promoters and sporting organisations barred TV cameras for fear of depleting attendances, and echoes of that battle continue intermittently today. But there was an inducement to televise sport when TV hours were restricted, because outside broadcasts, provided they were of events organised by bodies other than television, were, within certain limits, exempt from the total of permitted hours, so sport on television grew.

Some sport is disappointing on the small screen. Motor racing, for example, loses impact; the cameras appear to slow the cars when showing them head on, and the pungent smell of fuel and the shattering noise of engines are also missed. Other sports televise well. Motorcycle scrambling is one; show jumping is another, and TV coverage helped promote it long before Princess Anne took it up. Snooker was popular even in the days of monochrome television, despite the impossibility of telling the colour of the balls. Rallycross, a combination of motor racing and autocross, was actually invented for television by a *World of Sport* director.

Exclusive rights

Today, it seems, the public cannot be given too much sport. In recent Olympic Games and World Cup football years the BBC plumped for

* *BBC Handbook*, 1976.

lengthy coverage, dropping regular programmes to show every event live, while ITV, not unreasonably anticipating a feminine rebellion against a surfeit of sport, adopted the line, 'Your favourite scheduled programmes as usual, plus highlights of the sport later.'

In the event, the public opted for live coverage (and some of them for the recorded highlights as well). After the Mexico Olympics in 1968, in which the BBC's policy scored heavily, a Corporation executive rubbed in the fact with a telegram to his opposite number at ITV which said, 'The important thing is taking part, not winning. . . .'

Normally the two compete with each other to buy exclusive rights to televise sporting fixtures, but there are certain national events that cannot be acquired exclusively but which neither organisation had in the past been prepared to leave to the other: the FA Cup Final, the Derby, the Grand National, Wimbledon tennis, Test cricket and the Oxford and Cambridge Boat Race. The BBC transmits all six and has rejected proposals by ITV that the two organisations should alternate coverage of them because it can get the bigger audiences (the public still tend to turn to the BBC for major sporting events as they do for State occasions and despite occasional triumphs ITV has never succeeded in altering this materially). So ITV now competes directly only on the Derby and the Cup Final. (The Boat Race has lost much of its popular following since the war and Test cricket and Wimbledon tennis occupy a great amount of air time and disrupt schedules, which worries ITV more than the BBC since it has only one channel compared with the BBC's two.) However, some co-operation has been established over international football matches, with one company providing live coverage and the other recorded highlights in turn.

The money involved in acquiring rights to show sport is large: the BBC and ITV together have been paying more than £1·5 million a year for football, but much more has been demanded by the League clubs, who say they had to spend more than £1 million to bring their floodlighting up to the standard required for colour television and modern close-up camera techniques. However, television's negotiators estimated that clubs could get millions more by selling advertising at the grounds appearing on television. For a new branch of the advertising industry has grown up to buy banner sites at sports stadia when television cameras will be there. Skilfully placed, facing a camera position, an advertiser's message can get great and comparatively cheap exposure on television during a football match.

In the sixties television jibbed when racing cars began to look like high-speed poster sites and refused to cover meetings at which such cars appeared, but eventually it was television that had to back down; too much money was involved. Since then advertising sites have spread to the corner posts of boxing rings and even to boxers' shorts.

Sports promoters claim that television does not bring unalloyed benefits: while it may create a greater interest in a sport, the televising of, say, a football match may keep at home fans who would otherwise be passing through the turnstiles of a local club.

Saturday programmes

Saturday afternoons are now devoted entirely to sport on both BBC1 and ITV and average audiences total about 12·5 million, fairly evenly divided, though *World of Sport*, produced by LWT for the ITV network, has claimed a higher share of viewers than BBC's *Grandstand* in recent years.

This Saturday afternoon allegiance to sport has developed only since the start of the sixties. In the fifties sport on Saturdays was confined to a tea-time results service; the rest of the afternoon was given over to programmes for women and children. When the BBC began *Grandstand*, ITV competed by showing films, but in 1965 it lured Eamonn Andrews from the Corporation to present *World of Sport*, backing him up with Jimmy Hill and Peter Lorenzo on football, John Rickman on racing, Ian Wooldridge on cricket and Freddie Trueman on a roving commission. Since then the action content of the programmes has increased and the chat has been reduced. Dickie Davies, who was originally Eamonn Andrews's holiday relief on

Eamonn Andrews introducing the first World of Sport

World of Sport, has taken over the chair while *Grandstand* is fronted by Frank Bough.

Both programmes begin before lunch with trailers for the afternoon's soccer: *Football Preview* on BBC1, and *On the Ball* on ITV. The Football League allows these twenty-five-minute programmes to show only five minutes of taped action. It seems more, but ITV's Brian Moore told me, 'A save by a goalkeeper takes two and a half to three seconds of screen time. In ten seconds we can show the whole build-up to a save. If a match has two goals in it we can show them both in twenty-five seconds with no problems.' Montage sequences of a star in action are built up from clips of about two and a half seconds each. The programmes close with classified results, but in between they differ in that the BBC tends to concentrate on one or two events in the mainstream of sport, such as swimming and rugby football, while ITV shows a greater variety of less common sports – more than thirty different kinds in a year including American and Gaelic football, stock car racing, canoe slalom and hurling.

Both networks show racing, of course, *World of Sport*'s attraction being the ITV Seven, which began at the end of 1969 and has been called the greatest gambling gimmick of the decade. Viewers place accumulating bets covering the seven races normally shown in an afternoon, and the biggest winner has been a Nottinghamshire woman who won £12,399 for a 10p bet. The BBC has since introduced its own special bet, the Triella, which involves first and second horses in three races.

The acceptance of this inducement to betting has been remarkable considering that until 1958 television pretended horse racing was a sport in its own right unconnected with bookmakers. Then it began giving the odds after a race was over, and three years later began to give gamblers the service they wanted – the prices in advance.

The last segment of *World of Sport* before the results is always forty-five minutes of wrestling. This has been criticised but it is popular, having an extraordinary number of middle-aged women among its fans, and a cut in its time for any reason brings *TVTimes* more letters of complaint than any other subject on television.

Soccer action is not seen on Saturday afternoons except for matches like the Cup Final, which are sold out in advance and held when other fixtures have come to an end. The main coverage of football, apart from occasional live matches in midweek, is in the BBC's *Match of the Day* on Saturday night and LWT's *The Big Match* on Sunday afternoon (though different regions of ITV may show their own programmes). Between them the ITV companies usually cover at least six matches every Saturday. The matches to be shown, however, are not allowed to be announced until after the turnstiles have finished spinning.

Brian Moore commentating on football for The Big Match

In midweek the BBC's *Sportsnight* is the main programme, covering a variety of sports. ITV, which had a similar magazine programme when it began in 1955, now concentrates its midweek sport on another session of wrestling. But it has had a unique series in *The Indoor League*, devised by Yorkshire Television, director Sid Waddell, after *World of Sport* had covered a darts final at Alexandra Palace. *The Indoor League*, presented by Freddie Trueman, former Yorkshire and England fast bowler and club comic, from the Irish Centre in Leeds, soon had an audience of six million for darts, table skittles, table football, shove ha'penny, arm wrestling and American pool.

Outside broadcasts

For pre-war outside broadcasts the BBC used a one-kilowatt mobile transmitter and an aerial mounted on a fire escape ladder to send pictures back to Alexandra Palace. By 1939 they had two outside broadcast units with a range of up to thirty miles. In 1938 the Derby was televised direct (with one camera) and a Test match versus Australia at the Oval; in 1939 the Boon–Danahar fight and the Boat Race.

Today's OB units represent about £300,000 each and sport programmes are their biggest users. For Saturday sport programmes an OB team sets out on Friday in a caravan of vehicles transporting portable transmitters and generators, cameras and sound equipment, sometimes videotape recording equipment and possibly even a pre-fabricated tower on which to mount a camera. The key vehicle is the scanner van – a mobile technical centre.

For the coverage of, say, a motor race at Silverstone, the cameras, probably half a dozen of them, will be set up on roofs, towers and tripods. There may well be another camera to be fitted to a helicopter. They are all connected by cable or microwave radio link to the scanner van, on the roof of which is a microwave dish aerial that will be turned to face a receiving dish somewhere along a route arranged by Post Office engineers to leapfrog the signal to the studio centre.

On Saturday morning the crews report early for camera rehearsals. The director takes his place in the scanner van before his monitor sets, one for each of his cameras and one to show the picture selected for transmission. Seated beside him will be his PA, vision mixer and sound controller, whose team may use highly directional microphones to pick up the noise of individual cars. A telephone will connect the director to the commentator in his box overlooking the track. The commentator has a monitor so that he can see the pictures being transmitted and also to help him describe what he cannot see unaided, for parts of the circuit will be concealed from him. He may well have assistants to check lap speeds and records for him.

At the studio the over-all director of the programme has his own battery of monitors showing Silverstone, the other venues of the day and the programme presenter in the studio, all the pictures that are available for his selection.

The instant replay of a goal in football, a try in rugger or a jump in ice skating is now an expected and valued feature of television cover-age but instant action replays as they are seen today came about only in 1968 with the arrival of the video disc. It can replay action at any speed from normal to still frame. It can be used to freeze a picture from normal speed (and this facility is often used to create title sequences).

Its main use is in sport (and there may be 300 replays during a five-day Test match) but 30 per cent of its bookings are for other types of programme including slow motion sequences of ballet.

The great advantage of the video disc is that when recording live action it retains only the preceding thirty-six seconds, which means that while the director has to act quickly if the relevant action is not to be erased, he has merely to speak to the video disc engineer on his two-way voice link and the replay can be switched into the transmission. For events that are videotaped before transmission, such as *Match of the Day* and *The Big Match*, there is no need to run the video disc during the recording because the disc can record from the videotape.

Commentators

In the fifties a television personality who broadcast commentaries on a wide range of sporting and other events assured me that a deep knowledge of a particular sport was not essential; what mattered was professional fluency. A good commentator, he claimed, could commentate on any subject. He has not been seen on television for many years now.

Today's commentators are specialists, and a good one, such as *On the Ball*'s Brian Moore, is highly respected in the game, even though he was never a noted player. It is also common to back up a commentator with a sportsman of unchallengeable authority and knowledge, such as retired heavyweight champion Henry Cooper who has appeared frequently on boxing programmes.

The use of professionals reached a new dimension at the time of the 1966 World Cup when both the BBC and ITV fielded panels of them. ITV's was particularly successful. Malcolm Allison, Derek Dougan, Pat Crerand and Bob McNab were on television talking football night after night with Jimmy Hill and Brian Moore, yet their enthusiasm never flagged for a moment and it communicated itself to viewers. Panels of pundits became an established concomitant of big sporting occasions, sometimes seeming more important than the event itself.

Jimmy Hill, the bearded ex-Fulham player and former manager of Coventry City, brought a new skill to television, that of the football analyst, dissecting matches for their tactics and drawing attention to good performances or blunders by players and officials. It was a blow to ITV when the BBC snatched him away in 1973.

Yet most of television's sport reporters and commentators have won personal followings. Racing expert John Rickman acquired his by raising his hat to viewers, which earned him the nickname of 'Gentleman John'. Rugby League's Eddie Waring became a popular subject for impersonators because of his contemptuous dismissal of minor injuries on the field, delivered in a uniquely soaring and swooping voice; Harry Carpenter, the BBC's lightly built and bespectacled boxing commentator, was featured in many verbal work-outs with the heavyweight Muhammad Ali, winning Ali's affectionate approval, 'You're not as dumb as you look, Harry.'

Chapter 7

Drama

It begins with a writer and an idea. He may conceive the idea himself and fashion it into a script to offer to the BBC or one of the ITV companies with drama departments or, if he is an established screen-writer, he may be offered the idea or a suggested storyline and commissioned to produce the script. But nothing exists and there can be no production until the script has been set down.

The writer's initial discussions about it will be with a script or story editor charged with finding material for certain drama slots: a series of single, unconnected plays; a series of plays on a particular theme; or a series with continuing characters. Almost certainly the script editor will require some rewriting. It may be that there is an inconsistency in the plot or characterisation; it may be that the play in its existing form calls for extensive filming on location and the producer's budget cannot run to the cost of those scenes.

The producer, the executive in charge of a series, is normally given an over-all budget, which has to cover the costs of script, cast, director, design and prop departments, graphics, transport and much more. If he spends lavishly on one programme he will have to save money on another, perhaps by using a small cast and simple sets.

When editor and producer are happy with the plot, characterisation, dialogue and other facets of the script, the producer sets a recording date some weeks ahead and books a studio. The script is printed and circulated to the servicing departments and to the director chosen by the producer. The director, usually a freelance, agrees to do the play and talks to the casting director about actors and actresses to play the parts. They may agree that one actor is ideal for a certain part but find from his agent that he will be unavailable; a second choice may be committed to a film until a certain date, so the director considers whether he can begin rehearsals without him. The casting director may suggest trying an unknown youngster seen in repertory.

Meanwhile the designer has planned the sets. Sketches are made and maybe a balsa-wood model. The lighting director works closely with the designer at this stage, and so does the costume designer to make sure there will be no clashes between costumes and upholstery. It may be possible to supply some of the clothes from the studio wardrobe; others will be designed in the studio or bought from shops. The director arranges the order of shooting, planning some location shots for the day before the move into the studios.

Rehearsals begin in a bleak church hall, for studio time is valuable.

The stage manager puts tapes on the floor to indicate the positions that furniture will occupy. On the first day of rehearsal the cast arrive in casual clothes, greeting friends, last encountered in other productions. The director introduces the play and explains how he sees the production. The cast then read the play together while the director's production assistant times it, perhaps finding that it is over-long. Producer, director and author confer and the necessary cuts are made.

Next day rehearsals begin in earnest; the actors are alone with the director and the stage manager, and will be for ten days or a fortnight according to the scale of the production. They rehearse the moves under the director's instructions while he fills out his camera script, which is the writer's final script superimposed with instructions for the camerawork, the close-ups, long shots, cuts and mixes.

In the construction shops at the studio centre sets are being assembled. Props are being located, some from the stores while others are bought or hired. Costumes are fitted and alterations made. Music commissioned for the production is recorded.

Finally, the cast move into the studio. The sets will have been erected and the lighting arranged before they arrive. The director leaves the cast for his control room above the studio where he will watch on his monitors, his link with the cast being by microphone to headphones worn by the stage manager.

The first rehearsal is a 'stagger' – a run-through – interrupted for changes of position and new instructions. There may be another before the dress rehearsal in costume and make-up. Publicity 'stills' are usually taken at this time. Then it is time for recording. The cameras are lined up again, the floor manager cues the 'beginners', the action starts – and stops again because a camera is slightly off position. The action restarts and the play is performed. At the end the floor manager asks the cast to wait for a few minutes while the director checks the videotape. Then, 'OK studio, thank you everyone.' The lights dim, the cast remove their make-up, change into their own clothes and adjourn to the pub next door for farewell drinks in an end-of-term atmosphere.

There is still editing of the tape to be done; sound may be added or deleted and post-production effects incorporated. Then the show is ready for transmission and the studio publicity machine goes to work.

In the case of an ITV programme there is one more task remaining: a cast list is forwarded to all the regions that will be showing the play. Commercials to be shown on the night will be checked against the cast list for it would please neither production company nor advertiser if – to take an extreme case – an actress were to be seen adding arsenic to a drink in a thriller and reappearing a moment later during a commercial break to recommend a brand of tea. In fact, to avoid confusion of any kind, the IBA forbids showing any commercials featuring television performers alongside programmes in which they appear.

Plays

At the BBC the drama group's output is divided into three categories: serials, series and single plays, each having eight to a dozen permanent producers. The amount put out under each heading is fairly similar, though the greatest quantity is of serials and the smallest of singles.

Basically, a serial retains the same characters and develops the story of those characters chronologically; a series has a nucleus of permanent characters but consists of self-contained episodes and involves them with new characters each week, though the divisions are sometimes blurred.

What is remarkable is that the output of single plays has remained so large, for no one could claim that the British public as a whole are devoted to the theatre. The majority never go to see a stage play and, outside the big cities, it is not easy to see a major production. In the three pre-war years of television the BBC transmitted 326 plays, but only 14 of them were specially written for television. There was no such person as a professional television dramatist; dramas were written for the theatre or the cinema.

In the post-war period plays fell into three broad categories. There were classics: Shakespeare's *Macbeth*, Jonson's *Volpone*, Sheridan's *The Rivals*, Congreve's *Love for Love*. There were plays from the West End theatre: Coward's *Blithe Spirit*, Maugham's *The Circle*, Mazo de la Roche's *Whiteoaks* and Charles Morgan's *Flashing Stream*. Then there were new plays. The BBC had formed a script unit to encourage new material for television. A big success was Frederic Knott's *Dial M for Murder*, first shown on television in 1952 and later adapted for the theatre, the cinema and for television again; but new plays were still in the minority.

Some plays were televised direct from a theatre; others were brought into the studio at the end of their runs on stage (for example, Rattigan's *Browning Version* and Bridie's *The Anatomist*). This helped to solve the problem of finding actors to work in television, for while everything was live they still feared it, though the invention of the prompter's cut-out, which enabled him to kill the sound while giving a prompt to an actor who had forgotten his lines, went some way to improving matters.

One snag was that television acting required new techniques. Stage actors were inclined to over-project in a medium in which emotion can be conveyed by the eyes alone; film stars were used to the camera close-up but unused to the continuous shooting of television compared to the short takes of the film studios, and the necessity for learning all their lines in advance.

The first actor to become a big television star was Peter Cushing, who appeared in sixteen plays at the rate of one a month after his debut in 1951.

When ITV began in 1955 its plays were still largely theatrical. Associated-Rediffusion presented *Hamlet*, and scandalised Shakespearian scholars by fading out the end for commercials. ATV began by subcontracting its plays to H. M. Tennant, the theatre group.

When ABC began *Armchair Theatre* in 1956 its first production was Dorothy Brandon's drama of medical ethics, *The Outsider*, starring Adrienne Corri and David Kossoff, and that was an adaptation of a stage success of 1923. Dennis Vance, *Armchair Theatre*'s first producer, an ex-BBC director, had no team of writers to call on and, though he later secured the first play for television by J. B. Priestley, he concentrated on revivals of stage plays and adaptations of novels. Television drama had still to acquire an image or style of its own; nevertheless Vance lifted his plays into the Top Ten.

Then in 1958 a forceful, restless Canadian named Sydney Newman roared into the ABC studios from the Canadian Broadcasting Corporation and proceeded to change *Armchair Theatre* and the whole of television drama with it. His revolution came on the heels of John Osborne's *Look Back in Anger*, staged at the Royal Court Theatre, which had brought a revolution on the stage. Out went cosy plays with French windows and libraries, comic domestics and 'Anyone for tennis?' lines. Newman wanted plays about contemporary life. He wanted plays about real people in provincial towns, people who worked in factories and shops and got dirty and had the sort of problems the majority of viewers might experience.

He sought new writers to give him what he wanted and adaptors virtually disappeared from the studios at Teddington. Some of the plays were criticised for poor writing and the words 'kitchen sink' became a common term of abuse. Newman was accused of sensationalism, but his plays were talked about and audiences rose. He acquired the first television plays of Angus Wilson, Harold Pinter, Robert Muller and Alun Owen. He presented new faces, such as those of Tom Courtenay, Tom Bell, Peter McEnery and Vivien Merchant. He built a team of individualistic directors, such as Philip Savile, Ted Kotcheff and John Moxey.

By 1963 the pendulum had swung, the public were growing tired of slices from real life. The cry from the suburbs was for stories with a beginning, a middle and an ending. Leonard White, who took over from Newman, set out to provide them. His policy was 'the story comes first'. So in the years that followed there were fewer first plays by new writers. There were more adaptations and he wooed mass audiences with such popular, headline-making names as Bruce Forsyth and Eleanor Bron in *The Canterville Ghost*. When he starred Harry H. Corbett and Donald Churchill with Diana Rigg (making her television debut) in Churchill's comedy *The Hothouse* in 1964, *Armchair Theatre* achieved a new audience record of 8·2 million homes.

By this time television single-shot plays were generally declining in popularity, and it seemed that the single play might die, except for big-budget, star-name productions. The mass of the public, ran the argument, wanted only to be entertained and amused and found series with known characters and familiar situations easier to follow. A single play demanded some mental effort, its quality was unknown until it was under way and it might turn out to be disturbing or unsettling, and it was more expensive to produce than an episode in a series with continuing cast and sets. The odds seemed stacked against it.

The number of slots for plays declined in favour of more old films (which offered international names and nostalgia) and more drama series (familiar faces and continuing themes). Plays were no longer the centrepiece of the evening's entertainment around which the schedule was built. Yet they were still the most publicised, most written about programmes on television apart from documentaries. Partly, of course, because no critic could write week after week about the continuing story of *Coronation Street*, but mainly because plays, whether comedy or drama, classical or contemporary, are concerned with ideas and with life and reflect recognisable human situations. It is because of this that plays have been among the most criticised productions on television, generally by viewers shocked by themes that they find unpleasant to think about. Nudity and swearing have also caused complaints.

Most of the rows in the sixties were aroused by the BBC's *The Wednesday Play*. The Corporation had by this time acquired new television writers such as John Hopkins (who moved on to single plays from scripts for *Z Cars*), Dennis Potter, David Mercer, Giles Cooper, Colin Welland, David Rudkin and William Trevor. Wednesday plays were contemporary and experimental. They tackled back-street abortion (*Up the Junction*), corruption and violence among building-site workers (*The Lump*), and political chicanery (*Vote, Vote, Vote for Nigel Barton*). They made extensive use of film shot in the streets to break away from the restrictions of time, space and continuous performance imposed by studios and tape recording.

The play with the most far-reaching effects was *Cathy Come Home*, by Jeremy Sandford, starring two comparative unknowns, Carol

Ray Brooks and Carol White in Cathy Come Home

White and Ray Brooks, as a pleasant but feckless couple sinking into squalor because of the difficulties of finding a home. There had been documentaries with a fictional style; this was fiction with a documentary style. Parts of it were unscripted and director Ken Loach shot it in London's East End from cameras in the backs of cars. Many viewers were unable to separate fiction from fact; its impact was phenomenal and Shelter, the organisation for the homeless, became one of Britain's best-supported charities.

A number of the producers and directors concerned with the Wednesday plays, including James MacTaggart, Kenith Trodd and Tony Garnett, who between them were responsible for all those mentioned above, then formed a freelance company and began to make plays for London Weekend Television in 1968, the first being actor Colin Welland's *Bangelstein's Boys*, the story of a rugger club's boozy weekend excursion.

The BBC's contemporary plays continued under the title *Play for Today*, while *Plays of the Month* showcased classics from *Julius Caesar* and *Hedda Gabler* to *Charley's Aunt* (starring Danny La Rue) and *The Adventures of Don Quixote* (starring Rex Harrison), which was made on location in Spain in 1973.

The future of the single play had become safe, even though the grouping of plays under generic titles such as *Thriller* or *Menace* to establish viewer loyalty was inescapable. As an exercise, I once drafted in a matter of minutes a synopsis, the only merit of which was that it could have been offered to nine separate anthology series of the time, *The Edwardians*, *Love Story*, *Blackmail*, *The Gamblers*, *Trapped*, *Seven Deadly Sins*, *Seven Deadly Virtues*, *Armchair Mystery Theatre* or *Mystery and Imagination*. It proved that almost any play qualified, or could be modified to qualify, under almost any title. The titles were unimportant and did not even guarantee plays of uniform style or quality. This would not matter except that when setting up such a series the producer turns to established writers for contributions and the opportunity for new writers to get their work on the screen is reduced. Yet it is a fact that producers and story editors are more delighted by the discovery of a new writer than by several competent pieces from established writers.

An anthology series such as Granada's distinguished *Country Matters*, consisting of adaptations of short stories by H. E. Bates and A. E. Coppard, is, of course, a different proposition.

Serials

Serials fall into two main groups: those of pre-determined length, such as eight parts, which include adaptations of novels; and those of indefinite length which include all the soap operas like *Coronation Street*, which has been running since 1960. Early serials on BBC

A scene from The Grove Family

television were mainly adaptations of classics – *The Pickwick Papers*, *Kidnapped*, *The Three Hostages* – and fell into the first category, though an early British soap opera was the BBC's *The Grove Family* in 1954, but after this it virtually left the field to ITV, apart from *Compact*, which concerned the staff of a women's magazine.

The first serial really to grip the nation came in 1952 when Michael Barry, the head of drama, commissioned Nigel Kneale, an ex-actor whose short stories Barry had liked, to write *The Quatermass Experiment*, a science fiction serial about an heroic space professor and monsters from outer space. Viewers were warned it was unsuitable for children and enjoyed the touch of fear. *Quatermass II* and *Quatermass and the Pit* followed, with first John Robinson and later Andre Morell as the hero. Quatermass spanned five years and was also the subject of feature films. The year 1952 also brought *The Broken Horseshoe*, the first of many ingenious crime serials by Francis Durbridge.

In the sixties the serial became a suspect form of drama at the BBC because of ITV's soap operas, including the American *Peyton Place*, but in 1967 Donald Wilson's twenty-six-part version of Galsworthy's *The Forsyte Saga* changed attitudes. It ran on BBC2, was repeated on BBC1 and repeated again. It brought personal triumphs for Eric Porter as Soames and Nyree Dawn Porter as Irene. It won 18·5 million

Frank Middlemass as the Russian Commander-in-Chief in War and Peace

viewers and gave the BBC a breakthrough in the American market, although no concessions had been made to a transatlantic audience.

The classic serial was given a new life. There was a twenty-episode adaptation of Tolstoy's *War and Peace*, with Anthony Hopkins as Pierre, which was eight hours longer than the longest film version ever attempted, and used the Yugoslav territorial army as extras. There were Sartre's *Roads to Freedom*, de Maupassant's *Bel Ami*, Balzac's *Cousin Bette* and Zola's *Germinal*.

Susan Hampshire, Fleur in *The Forsyte Saga*, went on to play Becky Sharp in *Vanity Fair*, Sarah, Duchess of Marlborough, in *The First Churchills* and Lady Glencora in *The Pallisers*, a twenty-six part serial in 1974 known at the BBC Centre as 'the twenty-six Trollopes'.

ITV has also had distinguished serials, notably ATV's lavish 13-part *Edward the Seventh* in 1975, just as the BBC has produced soap operas such as *The Brothers*, concerning the lives and loves of members of a family road haulage firm, but ITV is the more readily associated with open-ended soap operas. Its first big success in this field was *Emergency-Ward 10*, a hospital saga that began twice weekly in 1957 and ran for ten years. Sir Lew Grade later confessed that ending it had been one of his two big mistakes – the other was ending *Sunday Night at the London Palladium* – and in 1972 he introduced another twice-weekly medical serial, *General Hospital*.

Minnie Caldwell and Ena Sharples – two favourite Coronation Street *characters*

Emergency-Ward 10's success was eclipsed by that of the twice-weekly *Coronation Street*, which arrived in 1960, set in six terraced houses, a pub and a corner shop on the outskirts of Manchester. In Patricia Phoenix, unknown before she won the part of Elsie Howard (née Tanner), the Street's siren, it created British television's nearest equivalent to the Hollywood movie queen.

She left the cast in 1973 – the storyline had Elsie moving to a new job in Newcastle-upon-Tyne – but *Coronation Street* continued and still included five of the original cast, although the serial had by then employed some 600 artists, 60 writers and 50 directors. Elsie returned in 1976.

Crossroads, set in a motel, began in 1964 because ATV needed a Midlands-based equivalent of Granada's Northern-based *Coronation Street*. It was seen four days a week and so, although it started four years after *Coronation Street*, it reached its 2,000th episode in 1973 when the *Street* was only on episode 1,330. Critics panned it and until 1972 it was not fully networked. Once it was, it topped *Coronation Street* in popularity polls.

Noele Gordon, its star, had previously acted as hostess of a Midlands-only programme called *Lunch Box*, and by the seventies it was claimed that she had made more television appearances than any other actress in the world. She complained, 'The critics don't understand the hard work that goes into it. If you were not a professional you would not last five minutes in it.' This was true. The late Jimmy Hanley, who played in it for some time, told me that at first it was all he could do to memorise new lines each day.

In 1972 de-restriction of television hours brought new programmes for women in the afternoon, including Yorkshire Television's *Emmerdale Farm*, a twice-weekly serial set on a small dairy farm in the dales.

Series

Western series have been popular on television from the early ITV days of *Gunsmoke* with James Arness, through to *Alias Smith and Jones*, which was inspired by the film *Butch Cassidy and the Sundance Kid*. Medical series enjoyed a vogue at one time with America's *Dr. Kildare* and Scotland's *Dr. Finlay's Casebook*. But, among series, nothing succeeds quite like crime.

Scotland Yard series have ranged from *Dial 999* and *Stryker of the Yard* in the early days of ITV to the more recent *New Scotland Yard* and *The Sweeney*. Detectives and gang busters have come in every shape and variety: *Maigret* (Parisian), *Cannon* (fat), *Kojak* (bald), *Ironside* (in a wheelchair), *Sergeant Cork* (Edwardian), *Peter Wimsey* (aristocratic), *Public Eye* (seedy), *The Saint* (freebooting), *The Expert* (medical), *Father Brown* (clerical), *Special Branch* (political), *Hunter's*

Leather-suited Honor Blackman in The Avengers

Jack Warner as Sergeant Dixon and Peter Byrne as Andy Crawford

Walk (provincial), *Riviera Police* (Mediterranean) and *Redcap* (military).

There have also been the representatives of secret services, as in *The Avengers*, *Callan* and *Spy Trap*, and innumerable court-room dramas from *Perry Mason* (American) and *Crime of Passion* (set in France) to *Six Days of Justice* (set in magistrates' courts) and *Crown Court* (using a jury drawn from the public to render an unscripted verdict on the evidence).

The longest-lived police series has been *Dixon of Dock Green*. Dixon was created by (Lord) Ted Willis for the 1950 film *The Blue Lamp* and was shot dead by Dirk Bogarde after twenty-one minutes of screen life. Willis resurrected him for television in 1955 and Dixon, played by Jack Warner, carried on until 1976, the oldest policeman in the force, epitome of the kindly, honest, old-fashioned copper.

ITV's answer in 1957 starred Raymond Francis as Detective Inspector Tom Lockhart in *Murder Bag*, which became *Crime Sheet*, which in turn became *No Hiding Place*, with Lockhart risen to the rank of Chief Superintendent. Francis played Lockhart for nine years, then the show was killed, but was brought back by public demand for another year, before being ended finally in 1967.

By this time there was a BBC series that changed not only crime shows but series in general. *Z Cars* was born in 1962 out of a documentary on police interrogation methods. Elwyn Jones, then assistant head of BBC drama, and scriptwriter Troy Kennedy Martin set it in a fictional version of Liverpool in which Seaforth became Seaport and Kirby New Town became Newtown, and it opened with a north-country folk song speeded up into a jaunty march.

Its front runners were four young policemen in patrol cars backed up at the station by Detective Inspector Barlow and Detective Sergeant John Watt. It concentrated on the minutiae of police work. Murders were comparatively rare; drunks and wife beaters and petty thieves were commonplace. Its policemen were human – Lynch (James Ellis) flagged down a motorist to ask the result of a race and Steele (Jeremy Kemp) fought with his wife. They took time out while on duty to smoke and eat chips. They were not always gentle with suspects; they could bully as well as help the public, unlike the fatherly Dixon.

The realism affronted some; the Chief Constable of Lancashire withdrew the co-operation of his force but the audience went from nine million to fourteen million in a couple of months.

Z Cars gave birth to *Softly, Softly*, with Barlow (Stratford Johns) and Watt (Frank Windsor) promoted to a regional crime squad, while *Z Cars* continued with new players. *Softly, Softly* gave birth to *Barlow at Large*, in which Barlow was attached to the Home Office.

Over the years almost all manner of jobs have provided material for series. *Harpers West One* was set in a big store, *Market in Honey Lane* in a street market. *Family Solicitor* and *The Main Chance* starred lawyers. *The Onedin Line* was set on a Victorian merchant schooner and *Warship* on a modern frigate.

Phenomenally successful in the sixties was ITV's *The Plane Makers*, though it began badly as a series about factory workers making an aeroplane. When Patrick Wymark was brought in as John Wilder, managing director of the firm, the action shifted to the boardroom and the public became fascinated by the writers' views of the big business jungle. Wilder was the man viewers loved to hate – aggressive, overbearing, rude, dynamic. In Wilfred Greatorex the series had the toughest of script editors, spending sometimes days in conferences over one episode. The series moved on into politics in *The Power Game*, with Wilder knighted. The BBC's answer was *Mogul*, which became *The Troubleshooters*, with Geoffrey Keen as Brian Stead, the driving managing director of an oil company.

Yet the most immediately successful series ever, which began in 1973, was a series without glamour, virtually without women, set in the confines of a prisoner-of-war camp. *Colditz*, with Jack Hedley, stiff-upper-lipped as the Senior British Officer, soon had an audience of sixteen million viewers.

Most actors welcome the opportunity to appear in a long-running series; it brings them as much security as an actor can know. And yet it worries them, for there is always the bogey of becoming typecast, of becoming so identified with one character that it is difficult to re-establish oneself in different roles. It happened to Rupert Davies of *Maigret*, to Raymond Francis of *No Hiding Place* and to Jill Browne, who played Nurse Carole Young in *Emergency-Ward 10*. However, Bernard Hepton was able to move from playing the German Commandant in *Colditz* to the television-addicted husband in the comedy series *Sadie, It's Cold Outside* and to a gallery of other roles in plays without any problem.

Chapter 8
Feature films

In a typical week there are fourteen made-for-the-cinema films on British television – six on BBC1, three on BBC2 and five on ITV. Because their length is greater than that of most television programmes they occupy major areas of the programme schedules, and at Christmas and on Bank holidays they are given even more peak-time.

Films are popular with the programme controllers because acquiring them is cheaper than making original television productions, yet they can win audiences of up to twenty million and figure in the Top Ten charts.

They are popular with the public because they bring to the small screen such international superstars as Paul Newman, Frank Sinatra and Marlon Brando. Generally, their camerawork is glossier, their location scenes and studio sets more lavish and their crowd scenes more heavily populated than those of television productions, because their budgets are vastly bigger and they are longer in the making. On top of this, the films of a decade or so back revive memories for viewers at home, who are older on average than the cinema-going audiences today.

TV Times and *Radio Times* and newspapers publish special columns on the films on television. There are paperback books giving concise details of films that may be seen on television. Yet films have not always enjoyed this popularity. In the early fifties the BBC still regarded them largely as being 'handy for emergencies when, for instance a sporting fixture is cancelled because of weather'.*

In fact, the major film distributors resisted the sale of films to television and were backed by many stars who were not keen on having examples of their immature work on view. Resistance cracked in 1963, as chill winds blew through Hollywood and cinemas in Britain were turned into bingo halls and bowling alleys, when Paramount offered a library of 700 pre-1948 films to television. Further sales followed.

For some time the showing of films on television was treated with reserve both by the television companies and the public. Because films released to television were at least five years old, they were referred to disdainfully as 'old films' and they were little publicised. The editor of one ITV programme journal explained to me at the time that if he created too much interest in 'feature films' (as the companies prefer to describe them) he might encourage people to return to cinema-going,

* *Television Story* by Frank Tilsley (BBC).

when his duty was to persuade them to stay at home and watch television.

Gradually, however, the number of films on television grew, within limits imposed by the BBC and the ITA (now the IBA) for the sake of programme balance. The IBA restrictions today permit a maximum of seven films in a week – subject also to another IBA rule that not more than 14 per cent of the week's viewing may be foreign material. The BBC observe roughly similar limitations.

However, the major distributors have maintained their ban on the sale of films less than five years old, for fear of causing further depletion in cinema-going, and there was a storm when producer Jules Buck made his film *The Ruling Class* starring Peter O'Toole available to the BBC in 1974 when it was only two years old. Other film men were angry because foreign-language films are normally the only ones that escape the five-year ban, and foreign films, though dubbed or sub-titled, are not popular with the mass of British viewers and are not often shown except by BBC2, which has screened some distinguished Continental films.

But the fact that a film cannot usually be acquired by television until it is five years old does not mean that all films become available automatically after their fifth anniversary. Companies will not release them to television while they are still capable of filling cinemas, and Robert Donat's *Goodbye Mr Chips* (made in 1939) and Clark Gable's *Mutiny on the Bounty* (made in 1935) were not made available until the seventies.

Packages

Films are generally released to television in packages. The distributors operate this system because it enables them to dispose of pictures that no company would seek to buy individually. To obtain some films that will win high audience ratings – like *Reach for the Sky* or *The Best Years of Our Lives*, which were viewed by twenty million – the TV companies also have to take a quantity of pedestrian ones, though packages offer the advantage of making it easier for them to build seasons or series of films showing the work of a particular star, such as *Wayne in Action*, or films of a particular type, such as *The Friday Western*.

A typical package has, in the past, comprised seventy-five or eighty films at a price of £500,000, working out at less than £7,000 a picture and £4,000 an hour – a mere fraction of the cost of an original drama production. But in 1975 the average cost of a film had risen to £10,000 and a popular Western could cost double. When ITV succeeded in buying six James Bond films in 1974 it paid a record £850,000 for them and had to agree not to show the first one, *Dr No*, until 1975 and the others at yearly intervals afterwards. Even this failed to placate some members of the film industry who called for a special levy on all cinema films screened, with the money going to the National Film Finance Corporation.

However, many films may be shown more than once during the five or seven years for which transmission rights are usually granted and some have been shown two or three times on the rival channels.

The BBC and ITV bid in open competition for the packages and between them usually hold about 3,000 films, but the use of films differs. The BBC shows its films throughout the country: ITV seldom does, except at Christmas and Bank holidays. The reason lies in the regional structure of ITV as a federation of companies that draw up their own programme schedules (subject to IBA approval). The 'slots' available for films vary from company to company, so ITV's films are held in a central bank from which the companies draw as required, observing an ITV system of coding which classifies films as suitable at any time (SAT), after 7.30 p.m., after 9 p.m. and after 9.30 p.m. The certifying of time suitability is the responsibility of the first company to transmit a particular film. The companies pay for them according to their share of the ITV audience.

The BBC, with comparatively few regional variations in its pro-gramming, can be flexible in allotting time for films and rarely finds it necessary to cut them. The ITV companies, leaving and rejoining the rest of the network at different times, but with certain immovable programmes like *News at Ten* on weekdays, have problems in fitting films of the right length to the slots available. Nevertheless, an advan-tage claimed for the ITV system is that companies can allow for regional tastes in their choice of films, for it is possible for a film to be a success in, say, Scotland but to cause yawns in London.

Suitable slots are normally of 90 or 120 minutes, with time for commercials to be taken out of this, but films are rarely obliging enough to run to exactly the length required. To screen a film that is short for the slot means filling out the remaining time with a cartoon or trailer; to screen a film that is too long for the slot means cutting.

Some years ago cuts could be quite brutal. *Scott of the Antarctic* and *The Cruel Sea* were shortened by twenty-nine minutes each. In one showing of *To Have and Have Not*, the most famous scene – the one in which Lauren Bacall tells Humphrey Bogart 'If you want any-thing just whistle' – was deleted. But after analysing 570 screenings in 1971 the IBA declared that the average cut was seven minutes and claimed that the cutting was done so skilfully that few viewers were aware of it. They said that complaints about cutting had become rare and these came mainly from film enthusiasts who are opposed on principle to any cutting.

Problems

A curiosity of the showing of films on television is that they occupy less time than they did in the cinema. This is because the standard frame speed of cinema films is twenty-four frames per second, but Western European television works on the principle of twenty-five frames per second. So on television, films are speeded up to synchronise with the twenty-five f.p.s. formula. Therefore a twenty-five-minute film runs for only twenty-four minutes on television or, more realistically, a hundred-minute film is transmitted in ninety-six minutes.

Another problem in showing films on television arises with widescreen processes such as CinemaScope movies. They are more than twice as wide as they are high, whereas the television screen is almost square, and to show them in their original proportions would mean merely a strip across the centre of the screen and a blank space above and below. Overcoming this and utilising the full screen area requires 'scanning' of the picture, i.e. selecting a portion of it to be shown. For example, in a dialogue between two people at opposite ends of the screen, it is desirable to select the part of the picture showing the speaker, eliminating the listener if necessary. This is achieved today by the making of 'rationalised' prints for television in which the pictures are re-cut and reduced to a standard ratio.

But the main problem over films is that television has been using more than 700 a year and many films made recently have included so much sex and violence that they are unlikely to be acceptable for peak-time viewing on television, with its family audience, even in five years' time when they become available. Already the distributors have made available a number of films that, although five years old, had never achieved a general release in British cinemas for various reasons. The BBC acquired ten such films in 1972, among them the science fiction picture *Fahrenheit 451*, starring Julie Christie and Oskar Werner.

A new industry was hailed when Hollywood began making films primarily for showing on television. An early example was *Madame Sin*, starring Bette Davis, which was shown on American television and later in European cinemas. But the 'films for television' business in Hollywood then turned over to programmes like *Columbo* with Peter Falk and *Banacek* with George Peppard, which were essentially television-type series of ninety-minute dramas.

British companies began making films for television too, an early example being a 90-minute drama, *The Prison*, transmitted by Thames Television under the title *Armchair Cinema*. Then London Weekend Television financed Peter Hall's film *Akenfield* and it was premiered on television and in the cinema simultaneously. The BBC also moved into financing films, the first being *Brother, Can You Spare a Dime?*, a compilation of newsreel and Hollywood material on the Depression, which was shown by the BBC four days before its cinema premiere.

The threat of a shortage of made-for-the-cinema films was not removed, but television and the film industry moved closer together, opening up the possibility of greater co-operation in the future.

Peter Falk (left) with Dick van Dyke in a Columbo *story*

A scene from Akenfield

Chapter 9
Light entertainment

What most of the public want most of the time from television is to be entertained, and many viewers say so indignantly in letters to the Press when regular entertainment programmes are cancelled or postponed at the time of a general election or other national crisis. Light entertainment departments make no pretence of providing anything more than entertainment, yet the heads of light entertainment are probably the most worried men in television. No other departments devise so many new series and in no other sector of television is the failure rate so high. It is as difficult to predict which comedy series will succeed as to forecast which records will top the hit parade charts, and that is one of the reasons for the development of try-out series like the BBC's *Comedy Playhouse* in which pilot episodes for series can be tested as single shows. If reaction is encouraging a series will follow; if the single programme flops then no more will be heard of it.

The public demand novelty and remain loyal to the familiar. The BBC's Edwardian music hall, *The Good Old Days*, chaired by Leonard Sachs, began in 1953, yet in 1975 it had a waiting list of 24,000 people anxious to don shawls and bonnets, blazers and boaters to bellow old songs and wallow in what Arthur Askey has termed 'instant mothballs' by forming the audience at the City Varieties in Leeds. This was enough to stock the audience for another twelve years.

Many shows killed off after long runs have been revived years later, either because of continued public demand or because nothing better had been devised. This happened with *This Is Your Life*, *What's My Line?*, *Sunday Night at the London Palladium* and *Candid Camera*. These shows illustrate something of the range that makes up light entertainment. It includes variety, musicals, comedy shows, quizzes, panel games and some programmes that defy categorisation.

Variety

The first programme to be televised from Alexandra Palace after the opening ceremony in 1936 was a variety show, but the early variety programmes were modest affairs. Budgets were small, impresarios were reluctant to release artists to a new medium that might take people away from theatres, and artists were not anxious to squander routines that could serve them for a decade in the halls.

After the war budgets were still modest and artists were still reluctant, but the BBC began to give variety more ambitious settings. The cabaret format was popular and Saturday night series included

A Swiss act in Café Continental *in 1948*

Rooftop Rendezvous (ostensibly set in a night club's roof garden) and *Café Continental*. Small-part actors played the audience, which was sometimes salted with a celebrity or two for whom at some stage in the evening an actor-waiter would open a bottle of television champagne amid the release of balloons and the hurling of streamers. The entertainment relied largely on Continental jugglers, acrobats and clowns with a six-girl chorus line.

There were also revues. Jack Hulbert agreed to a television version of *Here Come the Boys*, after it had run in the theatre for eighteen months, and this led to a series, *The Hulbert Follies*.

The biggest variety shows however were the Christmas parties in which actors sang, male announcers acted and girl announcers unveiled their legs in pantomime and delighted the audience at home with their unexpected jollity and amateur talents. Then ITV arrived and among the programme companies' chiefs were showmen like Prince Littler, Jack Hylton, Val Parnell and Lew Grade. These men could deliver the biggest stars in the business and they did.

ATV's *Sunday Night at the London Palladium* was the biggest variety series seen on television. Gracie Fields and Guy Mitchell were the stars of the first, sharing the billing on 25 September 1955 for an audience estimated at 387,000 – but then ITV was only three days old and still confined to London. By January 1960 Cliff Richard was singing to an audience of 19·5 million and later in the year Max Bygraves drew 21 million and Harry Secombe reached 22 million. The average audience stabilised at seventeen million and the show was a twentieth-century rite determining the Sunday evening habits of almost half the population. 'It's no use hiding the fact that *Sunday Night at the London Palladium* is more popular than going to church on a cold winter's night,' said a Woking vicar philosophically as he brought forward his evensong by half an hour.

Sammy Davis, Danny Kaye, Judy Garland, Bob Hope . . . virtually every big star in the world appeared at the Palladium and the compere's job made stars of Bruce Forsyth, Norman Vaughan and Jimmy Tarbuck. The show ran for twelve years, with breaks during the summer months, until 1967. Sir Lew Grade later regretted ending it and in 1973 brought it back with Jim Dale as compere, but the magic had gone.

The biggest variety show today is the annual *Royal Variety Performance* staged in aid of charity, with the television rights allotted alternately to the BBC and ITV. But variety shows on television were largely superseded by the arrival of 'the Show', such as *The Andy Williams Show*, *The Val Doonican Show* and *The Max Bygraves Show*. Instead of reserving his appearance until the end, the star (who might be singer or comic) acted as host, introducing his guests with plugs for their new records and forthcoming television shows (in which he would probably be a guest a few weeks later). He would also join his guests in duets and comedy sketches – it was a more integrated approach.

Comedy

Among the post-war comedy stars of BBC Television were Terry-Thomas and Norman Wisdom (who both moved on to films), Bob Monkhouse, Benny Hill and Arthur Askey, whose *Before Your Very Eyes* caused a sensation when it introduced Sabrina (real name, Norma Sykes) whose outstanding attribute was her bust.

In the sixties comedy shows underwent a series of revolutions. The BBC satire era, which began in 1962 with *That Was The Week That Was*, established new comedy stars in David Frost, the two Ronnies (Corbett and Barker), William Rushton, John Bird, John Wells, Eleanor Bron, Roy Kinnear, Roy Hudd and others. More importantly, it introduced a bite to television humour by enlisting writers from beyond the normal range of gag compilers. Playwrights, novelists and journalists contributed material that was sometimes juvenile and often savage. Targets included named politicians and businessmen, and though wife and mother-in-law jokes continued (and Les Dawson later rose to fame on them) taboos were ended so

Benny Hill, a long-time comedy star of television

John Cleese performing silly walk in Monty Python's Flying Circus

that Dave Allen could joke on BBC2 about priests and the confessional, death and funerals.

Rowan and Martin's *Laugh-In*, imported from America, brought faster, slicker sketches and throw-away gags, paving the way for quick-fire comedy such as Granada's *The Comedians* with thirty edited minutes of stand-up comics. *At Last the 1948 Show* in 1967 brought lunatic humour from John Cleese, Graham Chapman, Tim Brooke-Taylor and the lovely Aimi MacDonald and started a new trend. Cleese and Chapman joined Michael Palin, Eric Idle and Terry Jones from the children's show *Do Not Adjust Your Set* to produce the surrealist *Monty Python's Flying Circus*, which created the Ministry of Silly Walks and the panel game in which Marx, Lenin, Mao and Guevara were asked to name the year in which Coventry City had last won the FA Cup.

Tim Brooke-Taylor joined Graeme Garden and Bill Oddie in *The Goodies*, which was almost as anarchic and often more visual, one of its classics being a sequence in which mechanical excavators were seen snapping and savaging like prehistoric monsters, another when low-flying geese dropped golden eggs that skipped towards their targets like the bouncing bombs of the RAF's Dam Busters. Yet, despite the new trends in humour, the more traditional Morecambe and Wise were the nation's best-loved comedians at the start of the seventies.

Morecambe and Wise

Television's most prolific output of comedy, however, is in situation comedy, a curious form of screen drama in that it is usually recorded with a studio audience whose laughter robs a show of reality, but is believed to encourage viewers to laugh as well. There was a time when it was popular to feature artists playing television versions of themselves, as in the Bernard Braden and Barbara Kelly domestic comedies and *The Dickie Henderson Show*. But the briefest listing of some of the more easily remembered 'sit-coms' and their characters since then shows that subjects and settings are immaterial; what matter are the quality of the writing and acting. *The Army Game* had Alfie Bass and Bill Fraser as eccentric soldiers, *The Rag Trade* (Miriam Karlin as a militant garment maker), *Whack-O!* (Jimmy Edwards as a blustering headmaster), *The Worker* (Charlie Drake as an unemployable), *Mrs. Thursday* (Kathleen Harrison as a char who inherits a fortune), *On the Buses* (Reg Varney as a bus driver), *Father, Dear Father* (Patrick Cargill as the harassed parent of nubile daughters), *For the Love of Ada* (Irene Handl and Wilfred Pickles in love among the old), *Please Sir!* (John Alderton as the teacher of a problem class), *Dad's Army* (Arthur Lowe as the commander of a war-time Home Guard unit), *Never Mind the Quality, Feel the Width* (John Bluthal and Joe Lynch as two tailors, one Jewish, the other Irish), *Love Thy Neighbour* (Rudolph Walker and Jack Smethurst as co-existent black and white), *Up Pompeii* (Frankie Howerd as a Roman slave), *Some Mothers Do 'Ave 'Em* (Michael Crawford as an accident-prone incompetent). American-made series have added to the range.

The three shows that have made the biggest impact have been from the BBC, which caused the IBA to urge ITV light comedy chiefs to greater creativity at the end of the sixties.

The first of the three was *Hancock's Half Hour*, written by Ray Simpson and Alan Galton, which began life on radio in 1954 and moved to television in 1956. Tony Hancock played a dreamer puffed up by delusions of importance, despite an address in Railway Cuttings, Cheam, while Sidney James played a rascally friend; the results were such comedy classics as *The Blood Donor* and *The Radio Ham*. The series ran until 1961 when, at the height of his popularity, acclaimed as Britain's top comic, Hancock dissolved the team to strike out on his own in a search for new distinction, a quest that was sadly unsuccessful and that ended with his suicide in Australia in 1968.

When Hancock opted out, Galton and Simpson contracted to write ten different shows for the BBC's *Comedy Playhouse* series. Number four was about two rag and bone men, the son (played by Harry H. Corbett) another dreamer, the father (played by Wilfrid Brambell) dirty and dependent, thwarting his son's ambitions. The show led in

Tony Hancock

Wilfrid Brambell and Harry H. Corbett in Steptoe and Son

1963 to *Steptoe and Son*, which at its peak of popularity had an audience of twenty-two million.

Another series of *Comedy Playhouse* in 1965 yielded *Till Death Us Do Part*. Johnny Speight, who wrote it, had come from London's East End via scripts for *The Arthur Haynes Show*, which had run for nine years on ITV presenting Haynes as a tramp discomfiting authority personified by the smooth Nicholas Parsons. For *Till Death Us Do Part* Speight created Alf Garnett, one of the greatest characters in television history, a bald dock worker, ignorant, idle, selfish, lazy, jealous and bigoted. Garnett (played by Warren Mitchell) ranted against coons, Liverpudlians, the Labour Party and permissiveness; he was for the Queen, Empire, Church, Conservative Party and West Ham United. His language was coarse, and complaints poured in about the number of times he used the word 'bloody'. The irony was that Speight drew Garnett as a grotesque caricature to lampoon prejudice, yet many viewers listened to Garnett's outpourings with a degree of approval.

The number of writers like Speight capable of sustaining a viable output of comic writing has always been small; nowhere in television have new writers been sought so anxiously. Many of the best scripts have come from pairs of writers such as Galton and Simpson, Muir and Norden, Cooke and Mortimer, Esmonde and Larbey, Powell and Driver, and Clement and La Frenais.

Warren Mitchell as Alf Garnett

Musicals

When Henry Hall and the BBC Dance Orchestra appeared in the first week of television in 1936 it was considered sufficient to point the cameras at them and let them play, but in the post-war years a search began to find new ways of making music visual. In 1956, ITV's *Cool for Cats*, introduced by Kent Walton (who became better known later as a commentator on wrestling), used gramophone records of singers from Rosemary Clooney to Mario Lanza and provided a visual element by having a troupe of dancers to interpret the songs.

Then came the days of rock'n'roll and a twenty-six-year-old producer named Jack Good began a wildly successful series of pop programmes for teenagers inspired by the 1956 Bill Haley film *Rock Around the Clock*. His first was the BBC's *Six-Five Special* in which Josephine Douglas introduced the new stars and their hits, but a year later he moved to ITV to produce successively *Oh Boy!*, *Boy Meets Girls* and *Wham!!*

Teenage raves at the time, Cliff Richard, Marty Wilde, Billy Fury, Adam Faith and such eccentrics as the green-haired Wee Willie Harris were shown strutting, strumming and posturing, dramatically lit by spotlights or in silhouette. Good moved to America to make similar shows for television there (though he returned to England in 1964 to produce *Around the Beatles*).

Meanwhile, the pop bandwagon rolled on, through *Ready, Steady, Go!* and *Thank Your Lucky Stars*, striving ever harder for new effects. To allow maximum movement (and because many of the pop stars were incapable of producing the same sounds in a live session as in a recording studio) they generally mimed to their records. They were surrounded by studio mist (which tended to make them cough) and were projected as multiple images. Cameras zoomed, jerked and tilted; film sequences and abstract graphics were cut in or back-projected, and dancing spectators were made an integral part of the shows.

But there have been bigger audiences for less frenetic, squarer programmes such as *Billy Cotton's Band Show*, *Come Dancing* (ever popular despite send-ups of the tulle-and-sequins world of the Palais) and *The Black and White Minstrel Show*, with its top-hatted and black-faced singers and dancers, which won the Golden Rose of Montreux, the top international award for light entertainment shows, in 1961. And Eurovision made possible *A Song for Europe*, an international song contest estimated to have a world-wide audience approaching 500 million.

Games and contests

Other television contests such as panel games and quizzes fall into a category of their own, being mainly unscripted and unrehearsed. But even in talent competitions like Hughie Green's *Opportunity Knocks!*, which gave early television appearances to Mary Hopkin, Les Dawson and Freddie Davies, and in the *Miss World* beauty contests, drawing audiences of 23·5 million, the voting of the audience or the panel of judges was an unknown quantity until the end of the programme.

The heyday of the panel game was in the fifties and the most popular of them all – the most popular programme in the country at the time – was *What's My Line?*, the British version of an American show. It began in 1951 with Eamonn Andrews in the chair and a panel consisting of novelist Marghanita Laski, actress Elizabeth Allan, comedian's straight man Jerry Desmonde, and a man of many trades, Gilbert Harding. The object was simply to guess the jobs done by contestants, the best remembered of whom was a sagger maker's bottom knocker. The show grabbed the public's imagination in an extraordinary fashion. It was national news when panellist Barbara Kelly lost an earring under a chair and when Ron Randell blew kisses to women viewers and whenever Gilbert Harding lost his temper. The main reason many people switched on was in the hope of seeing the slumbering volcano that was Harding erupt over some misuse of the English language or at a misleading answer to a question, and regularly he did. The game ran for twelve years and was revived again in 1973 after a ten-year lapse, with David Jacobs in the chair.

From 1953 Eamonn Andrews also chaired the BBC's *This Is Your Life*, a programme difficult to classify, consisting of confronting an unsuspecting celebrity with relatives, friends and acquaintances (preferably people he had not seen for many years) and getting them to tell anecdotes about him while the cameras exposed his reactions and emotions. Clandestine planning enlisted the help of associates and families to decoy the subject into a studio for the moment of confrontation when Eamonn Andrews would step from behind concealment or remove a disguise to appear clutching a morocco-bound script and declaring, 'This is *your* life!' The series ran until 1964 and was resurrected by Andrews five years later on ITV. His faith was justified because it was soon the country's most popular show.

Another BBC favourite of the fifties was *Animal, Vegetable, Mineral?* in which distinguished archaeologists tried to guess the nature of exhibits from museums. The programme made a television star of Sir Mortimer Wheeler. Panel games continue, one of the seventies being *Call My Bluff*, a word game played between teams captained by Frank Muir and Patrick Campbell.

But when ITV opened in 1955 it introduced less gentle games. In *People Are Funny*, compered by Derek Roy, contestants were involved in practical jokes. In a typical example a woman was given a hammer and told to smash china wrapped in a cloth. She then found that it was

Bruce Forsyth compering Beat the Clock

from her own home. When the ITA asked for the show to be toned down ATV took it off.

Candid Camera followed, in which a concealed camera filmed the reactions of members of the public to having jokes played on them. Joker-in-chief was Jonathan Routh and the most famous hoax was the one in which a car was propelled into a filling station where the mechanic found, on lifting the bonnet, that there was no engine. But many of the jokes were cruel in that they were played on gullible members of the public and, although victims agreed to transmission of the film, it seemed sometimes that the programme's professionals were taking advantage of the niceness of ordinary people. After 6,400 hoaxes the programme died in 1967, though it enjoyed a revival in 1974.

In *Beat the Clock*, a segment of the original *Palladium Show*, the compere selected members of the audience, preferably honeymoon couples, to play games such as pulling on baggy trousers and welling-ton boots while keeping a balloon in the air. Prizes could reach £1,000. One of its most popular comperes was Bruce Forsyth who, in 1971, began to achieve audiences of thirteen million on BBC television with *The Generation Game* in which parents and children attempted activities less dependent on agility and dexterity than the Palladium

ones, but which still relied for entertainment on the readiness of contestants to allow themselves to be laughed at for prizes.

The lure of prizes played a big part in the early days of ITV. In its
first week in 1955 it introduced two quiz shows with cash prizes,
brought over from Radio Luxembourg. There was *Double Your
Money* in which Hughie Green offered £1 for the answer to a childish
question, doubling up to £32 for progressively harder ones, and leading to a chance of winning £1,000. In *Take Your Pick* Michael Miles
offered the key to a box as a reward for answering three simple questions, then harassed contestants with the choice of selling the key for
increasing amounts of cash or using it to open the box – where they
might find they had won an expensive suite of furniture or a gob
stopper. Both shows were criticised for promoting avarice and were
killed off in a drive for a new image for ITV in the second half of the
sixties, but Green and Miles were soon back with *The Sky's The Limit*
and *The Wheel of Fortune*, similar in style to their former series.
Meanwhile, ATV had introduced *The Golden Shot*, an electronic
archery game, also for prizes.

BBC quiz shows such as *Mastermind* and *Face the Music* were on a
different level, though ITV also had a respected quiz in *University
Challenge*, played by student teams from universities, under the chairmanship of Bamber Gascoigne, for nothing more than a trophy.

Yet, curiously, it was the BBC that developed the most extraordinary television contest of all in *It's a Knockout*, in which towns competed at glamorised versions of village fête games such as greasy pole
climbing, barrel walking, and tilting at buckets of water. It grew,
through Eurovision, into contests between countries under the title
Jeux Sans Frontières.

Chapter 10
Children's programmes

For better or worse – and opinions differ – children are voracious viewers of television. Those between the ages of twelve and fourteen are particularly addicted, averaging more than twenty-four hours a week.* And children, being naturally perverse, tend to prefer programmes other than those specially made for them. Question any group aged between six and fifteen about their favourites and the answers may well include *Z Cars* and *This Is Your Life*, *World of Sport* or even, inaptly, *Not In Front of the Children*. Reduce the age group to under-twelves, with earlier bedtimes, and children's programmes rate higher, but television's juvenile audience up to 9 p.m. and even later is still a substantial one.

For this reason programmes considered unsuitable for children are withheld until after 9 o'clock. Programmes before that time are meant to be suitable for all the family, though those actually designed for children fall mainly in the ninety minutes preceding the early evening news.

Some of these programmes have higher viewer ratings than adult ones: *Blue Peter* has attracted 40 per cent of five to fourteen-year-olds, while *Magic Roundabout* and *Watch With Mother* have reached more than 50 per cent of all children between two and four years old.†

The television organisations try to present what amounts over the week to a mini television service for children, a mixture of entertainment, information and ideas to encourage further activities in children of varying ages, backgrounds and interests. Since the 1972 derestriction of hours the BBC's output of children's programmes has grown to more than 700 hours a year, which is more than the time allotted to news, drama or light entertainment.

In ITV there is no over-all controller of children's programmes. But all fifteen companies have produced programmes for children, a total of as many as forty different series in a year, half of them networked, the others seen in one or more regions. This results in a wide range of programmes and the Network Planning Committee has a sub-committee to co-ordinate and supervise planning of the proportions of light entertainment, information, drama and nursery-age programmes.

Because of its potential influence, children's television has been one of the most discussed sectors of television and recommendations have come to the programme makers from all quarters. Probably the most frequently voiced concern has been about passivity induced in children

* Annual Review of BBC Audience Research Findings, 1975.   † *BBC Annual Report*, 1974.

by television; the call has been for programmes to stimulate them and involve them actively.

One thing that is certain is that there has been a steady move away from the furry animals and paper-folding that typified early programmes for children. When Francis Essex, ATV's Controller of programmes for the Midlands, introduced in 1974 a drama series called *Ski Boy*, filmed in Switzerland at a cost of £300,000 for thirteen episodes, he told the *Daily Mail*:

> Young viewers have become ever increasingly sophisticated in recent years. This is because they watch programmes made for adults and will no longer accept some of the styles of story-telling that would have passed five or ten years ago. Any author who consciously writes especially for children is probably doomed for disaster before he starts.

Doreen Stephens, who has headed the children's departments of both the BBC and London Weekend Television, has written,

> To give children a programme because *they* ought to see it or because *they* will be amused by it or entertained by it while it is boring to you is a discourtesy and condescension which deserves the treatment the children will mete out to it so long as there is something better to watch on the other channel.*

Annette Mills with Muffin the Mule

* *Evening Standard*, 22 October 1967.

So the makers of programmes for children have problems. In BBC Television's pioneering days they did not exist because there was no television at tea-time and the Corporation's efforts for children were concentrated on radio's *Children's Hour* presided over by 'Uncle Mac' (Derek McCulloch). Early television programmes after the war featured the puppet Muffin the Mule and the real animals of Holly Hill Farm, outside London, where Freddie Grisewood introduced viewers to the calves, ponies and sheepdogs. But faced with a choice of programmes on television or radio, children opted inevitably for television and *Children's Hour* was doomed, although its Toytown stories starring Larry the Lamb were later to be translated into animated films on ITV.

The paternalistic BBC television of the post-war era closed down every evening between 6 and 7 p.m. for what was known as 'the toddlers' truce'. The idea was that young children could be sent to bed at this time without arguments and older children could do homework without distraction. But the toddlers' truce ended in 1957, by which time ITV had arrived with filmed adventure series like *Robin Hood*, starring Richard Greene, *Sir Lancelot* (William Russell), *Ivanhoe* (Roger Moore), *Sir Francis Drake* (Terence Morgan) and a range of American-made programmes.

Information and light entertainment

Today's top two programmes for children are the rivals *Blue Peter* on BBC1 and *Magpie* on ITV, twice-weekly magazines with audiences approaching ten million. They retain the uncles and aunties of the old radio *Children's Hour* except that today's breed are young jetsetters travelling to countries such as Iran and Mexico, participating in activities from aqua-lunging to traction-engine driving, and sharing their experiences with their young viewers. Of course they are no longer called uncles and aunties; to children they are simply John, Peter and Lesley (*Blue Peter*) and Jenny, Doug and Mick (*Magpie*).

Both programmes are keen on animals. *Magpie* has featured a pony and *Blue Peter* a lion cub. They are both concerned about the environment. *Magpie* included a feature *Who Cares?*, which focused attention on noisy lorries and smoky chimneys, while *Blue Peter* ran a competition, *Operation Eyesore*, which invited ideas for transforming rubbish dumps and slag heaps and brought in 63,000 entries.

Both like to aid deserving causes. When *Magpie* asked for help in providing comforts for children suffering from the crippling condition of spina bifida, nearly £80,000 came in. *Blue Peter*, which appeals for goods rather than cash, collected enough unwanted paperback books to provide four inshore lifeboats and enough old wool and cotton to supply ten medical vehicles for use in West Africa.

Other information programmes on BBC have ranged from Patrick Moore talking about the stars to *Val Meets the VIPs*, in which Valerie Singleton, best known of *Blue Peter* presenters, introduced children to such celebrities as Margaret Thatcher and Morecambe and Wise. ITV series have included *If I Were You*, a discussion programme with a junior brains trust (ATV) and Southern Television's *How*, dispensing random information, such as the way in which a knight in armour was hoisted on to his horse and how Stonehenge was built.

Animal programmes have been featured on both networks, and the range of quizzes has included the BBC's general knowledge *Top of the Form* inter-schools contest and a natural history competition, *The Survival Game*, from Anglia.

Since 1955 the first name in light entertainment has been *Crackerjack*, the BBC's pint-sized version of adult variety, introduced originally by Eamonn Andrews and later by Michael Aspel. A pioneer among talent shows for children was *All Your Own*, which was introduced by Huw Wheldon, later to become managing director of BBC Television. Pop music has been provided by Granada's *Lift Off*, introduced by Ayshea Brough.

In comedy a trend-setting programme was the 1968 *Do Not Adjust Your Set*, produced by Humphrey Barclay, a Cambridge contemporary of David Frost and member of the Footlights revues. It starred Eric Idle, Terry Jones and Michael Palin (who had written material for Frost), Denise Coffey and David Jason and previewed the sort of madness that Idle, Jones and Palin were later to present to adults in *Monty Python's Flying Circus*.

Actors and puppets
Drama in children's television means mainly serials, though *Jackanory Playhouse* has presented single plays for six- to ten-year-olds by playwrights including Henry Livings. The BBC has adapted serials from well-known books such as *Tom Brown's Schooldays*, *Little Women*, *The Last of the Mohicans* and *The Black Tulip*. ITV has dramatised *Black Beauty*, *Redgauntlet*, *Black Arrow* and *Sexton Blake* but, after an appeal by the ITA in the late sixties for some fresh thinking in children's programming and for some new serials to replace repeats of *Robin Hood* and American space series, ITV introduced original serials which included *Catweazle*, the story of an eleventh-century magician in twentieth-century Britain, *Tom Grattan's War* (about a boy in the First World War), *Follyfoot* (centred on a riding stable) and *Arthur of the Britons*, a twenty-six-part HTV series that revised the image of King Arthur to that of a freedom fighter.

Drama's strangest phenomenon has been *Dr Who*, the BBC's saga of a double-hearted time lord travelling the planets and the centuries

John Abineri (left) as Chingachgook and Kenneth Ives as Hawkeye in The Last of the Mohicans

Tom Baker and Elisabeth Sladen in Dr Who

with youthful assistants in his Tardis, a converted police box. Its most remarkable feature is that it has continued since 1963 despite four changes of star. William Hartnell, the first Doctor, was succeeded by Patrick Troughton, who was followed by Jon Pertwee who gave way in 1974 to Tom Baker. They looked different and adopted different characteristics, but this was explained in the story by the fact that the Doctor is not from earth. One episode in the Pertwee era managed to include the two earlier Doctors as well.

The success of *Dr Who* has been largely due to the fanciful creatures the Doctor has had to fight. Ice Warriors, Cybermen, Yetis and Drashigs have menaced him, but the most popular have been the Daleks, gliding pepper pots reiterating mechanically, 'Exterminate! Exterminate!' Parents, many of whom have watched as avidly as youngsters, have complained that sometimes the monsters in the series have been too horrifying and children have looked away from the screen, but Terry Nation, the scriptwriter who created the Daleks in 1963, says, 'The answer is simple; kids love to be frightened.'

A success story of the sixties was the series of puppet thrillers that began with *Supercar*, was followed by *Fireball XL5* and *Stingray*, and reached a peak of popularity with *Thunderbirds*. The puppets were the most sophisticated ever seen. The twenty-inch tall stars of *Thunderbirds*, like Jeff Tracy, Lady Penelope and Parker the butler, cost £300 each and were suspended on wires one-5,000th of an inch thick. They and their table top vehicles, ranging from spacecraft to submersibles, were surrounded by realistic special effects involving the blasting off of rockets and the blowing up of buildings. The programmes cost £40,000 each, but the merchandising of the series was on a vast scale; there were books, comics, records and a wide range of toys headed by Lady Penelope's futuristic Rolls-Royce.

These programmes were the achievement of four film technicians, husband-and-wife Gerry and Sylvia Anderson, Reg Hill and John Reed, who had set up on their own in 1958 with £500 capital in a warehouse-studio soundproofed by 1,500 empty egg boxes nailed to the walls. They had never set out to work with puppets; it just happened that the first commission they could get was for a puppet film and then Sir Lew Grade, chief executive of ATV, decided to back them. But *Captain Scarlet*, which succeeded *Thunderbirds*, was less successful, and by then the Andersons were already planning new activities, filming television series like *Space 1999* with a blend of human actors, models and special effects for adult audiences.

Simpler puppets have been the mainstay of programmes for small children. There have been Tingha and Tucker, Pussy Cat Willum, Sooty, Andy Pandy, Torchy the Battery Boy, the Bumblys, the Flower

Sooty, Soo and Sweep with Harry Corbett

Pot Men, the Wombles, the Clangers and the characters of the French-made *Magic Roundabout*.

Story-telling programmes have also been popular. The BBC's daily programme *Jackanory* has had Rodney Bewes relating *The Wind in the Willows* and Ted Ray the story of *Thomas the Tank Engine*. The BBC has concentrated on this sector of children's viewing. More than two million toddlers, half the under-fives in Britain, watch *Play School*, shown five days a week since 1964, with Fred the hamster, Bit and Bot the goldfish, Benjamin rabbit and the dolls Big and Little Ted, Hamble, Jemima and Humpty. The part these programmes play in the lives of small children was demonstrated when the BBC dropped *Watch With Mother* to show cricket. Thousands of letters reached the Corporation from mothers complaining that their children had been left in tears and the BBC had to promise it would not happen again.

Chapter 11

Education

Many television programmes, particularly documentary and current affairs programmes, could be termed educational but, in a stricter sense, educational television means programmes in series with a clearly defined educational aim, planned in conjunction with educational authorities and teachers. These programmes include school and adult education series and Open University lectures. The first to start were school programmes in 1957.

Birth of school television

The man directly responsible for the start of school programmes was Paul Adorian, a radio engineer who became concerned with visual aids to teaching during the war, when he acted as adviser on special projects to the Air Ministry and invented a flight simulator. Immediately after the war he edited some film strips for instructors and was convinced of the value of visual aids in education.

He tried to interest the BBC in a service for schools, but although they carried out a closed-circuit experiment in Middlesex in 1952, school television was still a dream until 1956, when Adorian became managing director of Associated-Rediffusion, then ITV's London weekday programme company. One of his first acts was to have plans prepared for school programmes and at the end of the year his board gave formal authority for an experimental series.

Television staff were enthusiastic and so were the ITA. But the teachers. . . . Adorian recalled,

> Firstly they were suspicious of our motives; they feared we would use the programmes to advertise to children. When we said we would not carry any advertising in school programme time they were even more suspicious.
>
> Secondly they were frightened that we would make the teacher obsolete. In fact, our method was to be one of enrichment, helping the teacher by supplying him with aids he could not otherwise command.

Adorian drove ahead. Early in 1957 an Education Advisory Committee was formed under the chairmanship of Sir John Wolfenden, then Vice-Chancellor of Reading University, and the first programme was transmitted on 13 May.

That first programme, called *Looking and Seeing* and aimed at fourteen- and fifteen-year-olds, could be watched only in the London and Midland areas and it is estimated that a mere eighty schools viewed on what Wolfenden introduced as 'an important day in the history of TV in this country'. Furthermore, only a few of those schools had officially provided sets; the others used sets furnished by parents or teachers. So, over the next twelve months, Associated-Rediffusion gave 100 sets to schools and by the end of 1958 there were 1,000 schools watching the twice-daily teleclasses.

A term later, on 24 September, the BBC began a nationwide service for schools, and figures began to rise slowly. By 1963 they had reached 6,500; by 1964 they were 8,000 and by the end of 1965 they were 12,000, but after eight years of programmes for schools, two-thirds of the country's 38,000 schools were still not using them.

Adorian described his feelings to me at the time.

> I am disappointed that while over 90 per cent of the families in this country have a TV set, less than one third of schools have television. It is no good hiding behind financial difficulties. If the teaching profession were as go-ahead as it should be, every school should have at least one set and some should have two. This most valuable service which costs ITV and BBC together over £1 million a year * is not being fully utilised.

The major difficulty, apart from the antipathy of some teachers towards television, was that of fitting TV lessons, transmitted at fixed times, into school timetables drawn up by thousands of individual head teachers. This was the reason why every school programme was – and is – repeated at a different time. But this drawback became less important as video-recording machines became more readily available. The objection was removed when a school could videotape a programme and store it for showing when it suited the school. Recognising this, the BBC and ITV arranged copyright concessions in 1970 to enable schools to tape off-air and show the programmes at will within a year.

The advantages of this were two-fold. For with extra hours about to become available to television, the ITV companies wanted to switch afternoon time devoted to schools to programmes with potentially bigger audiences, particularly women at home. In 1972 ITV moved school programmes to the mornings, though the BBC, who could not recoup any money by adopting such a course, continued to transmit them mainly in the afternoons.

Nearly 30,000 schools now make use of television programmes and that is some 80 per cent of the total. About 31 per cent of secondary schools have videotaping facilities, a figure that rises to 53 per cent in the case of big schools – those with more than 800 pupils.† Yet the

---

* Now more than £2 million.   † *BBC Handbook*, 1976.

majority of schools still have only one television set, and a 1970 survey by the Department of Education and Science found that in many schools viewing conditions were unsatisfactory.

A pointer to the future is that the Inner London Education Authority have built a cable network connecting every ILEA college and school to their own Television Centre from which they can transmit not only BBC1, BBC2 and ITV programmes, but several extra channels of their own.

Programmes for schools and nurseries

School broadcasting is the area of closest co-operation between the BBC and ITV; there is no other in which the rival organisations disclose and discuss their plans so fully to avoid clashes. They also work in co-operation with the Department of Education and Science, with Education Advisory Councils and have their own Education Officers with teaching experience, who visit schools to channel advice to teachers and evaluate the response to programmes.

The first series from Associated-Rediffusion in 1957 included *On Leaving School* (for teenagers), *People Among Us* (on immigrants), *A Year of Observation* (the International Geophysical Year) and *The Ballad Story* (poetry).

Today, both the BBC and ITV have wide ranges of programmes for primary, middle and secondary schools. ITV's more recent series have

A school version of Macbeth *with Michael Jayston in the name part*

ranged from *It's Fun to Read* (an introduction to reading for four- to six-year-olds) to a special production of John Whiting's *Marching Song* for the fourteen-plus. BBC1 series have included *People of Many Lands* (geographical documentaries for ten- to twelve-year-olds), *Television Club* (for backward children of twelve to fourteen) and *Tout Compris* (a French language series for children of twelve to fourteen filmed on location in France). There are regional programmes for schools in Scotland, Wales and Northern Ireland.

Many of the programmes, particularly drama productions, have been of such a high calibre that they might well have been enjoyed by adults at peak time. In 1973, for instance, John Bowen wrote for the BBC a three-part modern version of *Julius Caesar* called *Heil Caesar!* which showed Brutus and Anthony (Anthony Bate and John Stride) making 'equal time' television broadcasts after Caesar's assassination. This was screened later as a single-shot play for adults. Other programmes have raised storms in Parliament and the Press: these have been on such subjects as childbirth, contraception, venereal disease and drug addiction, though there have also been programmes on the handling of money, on careers and on religious matters.

A new development at the start of the seventies was the pre-school educational programme (as distinct from play school programmes, which have been a feature of both the BBC and ITV schedules for many years). The move, which was accompanied by controversy, was brought about by an American series, *Sesame Street*. Its fifty-minute programmes for under-fives at home and in nurseries used the techniques of TV commercials, with fast-moving games and cartoons featuring friendly, fantastic creatures, to introduce them to letters and numbers. The series was exported to fifty other countries, but Monica Sims, head of children's programmes for BBC Television, rejected it as being 'too American, too middle-class and too authoritarian'. ITV took it up and experimental showings were arranged at the end of 1971 on HTV, Grampian and London Weekend while sociologists monitored reactions. Generally, children enjoyed *Sesame Street* and most parents approved of it, apart from some qualms about the Americanisms, but educationists quarrelled over the methods that should be used to teach young children and whether, in fact, it was desirable to attempt to teach them at all. However, *Sesame Street* galvanised activity in programming for pre-school children, and British programmes, using jingles, puppets and story-tellers, found their way on to both networks at the end of 1972.

Adult education

Education programmes for adults were inevitable after the establishment of the school service, but they did not begin until six years after it, in 1963. There were two main reasons why they were delayed: one was a fear that the word 'education' would keep sets switched off, and the other was the limited number of hours that television was permitted then.

There had been experiments despite the restricted hours. In 1960 Associated-Rediffusion transmitted *Chez les Dupré*, a French language series in London in the early evening. In 1961 the BBC put out *Science on Saturday*, and in 1962 Ulster Television screened late-night lectures on medicine, science, law, history, music and economics in association with Queen's University, Belfast.

Then, in July 1962, following the report of the Pilkington Committee, the government agreed to allow additional hours for television, providing these hours were used for adult education. The BBC and ITV produced a definition that declared, 'Educational television programmes for adults are programmes (other than school broadcasts) arranged in series and planned in consultation with appropriate educational bodies to help viewers towards a progressive mastery or understanding of some skill or body of knowledge.'*

Advisory committees were set up and the first programmes were launched by ITV in January 1963. They started on Sunday mornings under the title *Sunday Session* (thus avoiding the use of the word 'education') and there were three groups of programmes of twenty minutes each between 10 and 11 a.m. They were *You Don't Say* (spoken English), *Pen to Paper* (written English) and *Mesdames, Messieurs* . . . (for those who had learned some French at school). Results were encouraging. The average audience was 750,000 a week, nearly four times the number of full-time students in Britain. More than half of the viewers were under forty-five, most had left school at fifteen or sixteen and they were divided equally between the sexes.

The BBC began adult education programmes in October 1963, putting out five separate half-hour programmes weekly, at 12 to 1 p.m. on Saturday and 11.30 to 1 p.m. on Sunday with late-night repeats. The first six series were an introduction to the theory of relativity by Professor Hermann Bondi, an account of human biology, Italian for beginners, an introduction to European painting, a series on dressmaking and a keep-fit course. When BBC2 opened in 1964 it devoted one evening a week to education, under the title *Tuesday Term*, but when the 'Seven Faces of the Week' policy was changed the following year this was replaced by shorter items spread over weekday evenings.

Recent BBC and ITV series have been on collecting, home maintenance, golf, photography, community living, industrial safety and office management. Sales of some of the supporting books and booklets,

* *Broadcasting*, White Paper (Cmnd 1893) HMSO.

An adult education lesson in flower arrangement by Jean Taylor

particularly on hobbies such as dressmaking, driving and cookery, have been in the best-seller class.

The BBC has also carried refresher courses for doctors, courses on industrial relations for trade unionists and language programmes for Asian immigrants, while ITV has conducted local experiments, such as a Scottish Television postgraduate course for doctors and a Westward Television series for teachers of primary mathematics.

Open University

A major step forward in the use of television for education in Britain came with the establishment of the Open University, designed to enable students, particularly those of mature age, to acquire degrees by studying, mainly in their own homes, through radio and television broadcasts and correspondence work.

The Open University involves a partnership between the University authorities and the BBC, the University laying down the objectives and character of the programmes, the BBC staff – based at Alexandra Palace, the original television centre – providing the presentation and production skills and making the programmes. The service is paid for by the University from Department of Education and Science funds – the only part of educational television where costs are not borne solely by the broadcasting organisation.

Open University television lectures began in January 1971 with 25,000 registered students and countless eavesdroppers. At first there were four hour-long programmes a week, one for each of the first four courses; they were broadcast on BBC2 on Saturday and Sunday mornings with a repeat in the early evening during the week. By 1975 there were 50,000 students taking 78 courses, the number of programmes had risen to 300 a year and programme time for the Open University equalled the combined time of BBC school and further education broadcasts, effectively doubling the time the BBC allotted to education.

Chapter 12

Arts and sciences

Arts programmes may appeal only to minority audiences, but it is sometimes forgotten how large a television minority audience can be. It may look small compared to the audience for *Des O'Connor Entertains*, but *Omnibus* can attract a regular two million viewers, which is vast compared with the number who visit concert halls and art galleries.

And yet there are many who resent the showing of an arts programme at peak time as something of an intrusion. This was demonstrated in 1972 when the IBA suggested to the ITV programme companies that their proposed Christmas schedules were on the lightweight side and would be improved by the inclusion of Verdi's opera *Macbeth*, which Southern Television had recorded at Glyndebourne. The idea gained currency that the IBA wanted it shown as the main programme on Christmas night. *TVTimes* was inundated with letters from viewers declaring that what they wanted at Christmas was jollity, not morbid, highbrow opera. At the same time some wrote acclaiming the idea. Television provided little enough for opera lovers, they said; they did not begrudge the mass audience its light entertainment shows but why should others not have something to enjoy once in a while? In the event the programme was transmitted on 27 December and had an audience of two million, which would have filled all seats for a daily performance at Covent Garden six days a week for two years, and it seemed that a surprising number switched on to see what opera was like and many of them enjoyed it.

Until 1954, in fact, the BBC had not infrequently devoted the major part of an evening to opera, but after the arrival of ITV minority programmes tended to be shown out of peak hours. Recently, however, the BBC has been able to show such programmes at better times again because its two channels allow it to provide alternative viewing.

Magazine programmes

The series that did most to popularise the arts on television was the Sunday night magazine *Monitor*, which was launched in 1958. Huw Wheldon presented it in an avuncular manner that irritated some but he cut much of the mystique and pretentiousness from art. *Monitor* ranged over painting and ballet, music and sculpture, and most programmes offered something for everyone. The programme gave Sir John Betjeman one of his early television appearances, reading poems about London. It also introduced the work of several film directors who have since become famous in the cinema, among them John Schlesinger, John Boorman and the controversial Ken Russell. Russell had made only amateur films before he joined *Monitor* but his essays on the composers Elgar, Bartok, Debussy and Delius had the talked-about imagery and style that he transferred later to the wide screen.

Monitor's success encouraged other series, such as Mervyn Levy's *Painter's Progress* and John Berger's *Ways of Seeing*. Sir Gerald Kelly guided viewers around art galleries, causing a sensation in those pre-Garnett days when he described a painting as 'bloody marvellous'. *Monitor* was later succeeded by *Omnibus* in which a whole programme was normally devoted to one subject.

ITV's answer to *Monitor* in 1961 was ABC's *Tempo*, whose editors included Kenneth Tynan who interviewed Franco Zeffirelli and Truman Capote for the programme. It also showed Annie Ross and Yehudi Menuhin, Graham Sutherland and Marjorie Sigley, a Tottenham teacher whose expression classes in which she encouraged small children to improvise drama made such good television that she was provided with programmes of her own. ABC also produced *The Book Man*, the first British television series devoted solely to books and authors, among whom were Vladimir Nabokov, Nicholas Monsarrat, Somerset Maugham, Ivy Compton-Burnett and Dame Edith Sitwell. But neither series was fully networked and both died when ABC merged with Rediffusion to form Thames in 1968.

Sir John Betjeman in The Book Man

Tempo's successor was London Weekend Television's *Aquarius* introduced in 1970, edited and presented by Humphrey Burton, a former editor of *Monitor* and head of music and arts for BBC Television. His first programme included a sequence from French film director Jean-Luc Godard's *British Sounds*, which featured a glimpse of full-frontal nudity. From a fortnightly series, it became weekly in 1971 though, for nearly three years, it was pitted in London against the BBC's *Match of the Day*. Burton claimed it had no formula. Its one hundredth issue in 1973 included the music of Yehudi Menuhin and Edwin Roxburgh, the poetry of e. e. cummings and the horror films of Vincent Price. Burton also produced for LWT some major arts 'specials' including music programmes with Leonard Bernstein, Colin Davis and André Previn, before returning to the BBC as Head of Music and Arts.

Music and painting

Previn became the best thing that happened to music on television, which has always presented a challenge to directors, the chief problem being what to show while the music is being played. Previn, the fluent and witty principal conductor of the London Symphony Orchestra – he once appeared as a bus conductor in a Morecambe and Wise programme – was signed on a three-year contract by the BBC. In a number of programmes with the orchestra, as often as not dressed in informal rehearsal clothes, he showed a rare gift of popularising great music without debasing it.

The BBC, which has also shown Klemperer conducting all the Beethoven symphonies, and Ashkenazy playing all the Beethoven piano concertos, is a leading patron of music. It has twelve orchestras and employs a third of the country's full-time symphony musicians. It has organised the annual eight-week season of Henry Wood promenade concerts since 1927 and its televising of the last night of the proms has become an institution. It broadcasts from festivals and also commissions works – Benjamin Britten's opera *Owen Wingrave* was written specially for television.

ITV also supports the arts with grants to regional associations and festivals and covers a number of festivals from Edinburgh to Glyndebourne. It had one of Britain's most distinguished art historians and critics as the first chairman of the ITA in Sir Kenneth (now Lord) Clark. He made several series for ITV ranging from *Rembrandt* to *Great Temples of the World*, but his greatest television achievement, the monumental thirteen-part series *Civilisation*, which traced the work of writers, architects, painters, sculptors and builders across the centuries, was made for the BBC.

Films and film-making have regular programmes on all channels

Civilisation – *Kenneth Clark by a Celtic cross on the island of Iona*

and are inevitably popular because of their content of clips. At one time, apart from a Scottish Television series, *This Wonderful World*, presented by John Grierson, the pioneer documentary maker, they did little more than link together a series of clips with a theme and some flippant comments, but in general these programmes have now moved on to more serious discussion and presentation of the work of directors and artists.

Science programmes

There was a time when science programmes seemed designed more to entertain than to inform seriously. There were zoo programmes and the travelogues of Armand and Michaela Denis, but they did lead to Anglia Television's distinguished *Survival* series and to David Attenborough's jungle safaris. Leslie Hardern introduced the BBC's *Inventor's Club*, while on ITV Huw Thomas introduced *You'd Never Believe It*, an ABC series that investigated such acts as lying on a bed of nails and walking on hot coals, but they gave way to medical series typified by *Your Life in Their Hands*, which showed surgeons at work.

The space programmes of America and Russia did much to popularise science on television. When Neil Armstrong became the first man to walk on the moon in 1969 a small camera transmitted pictures to a ground station in America and the pictures were relayed

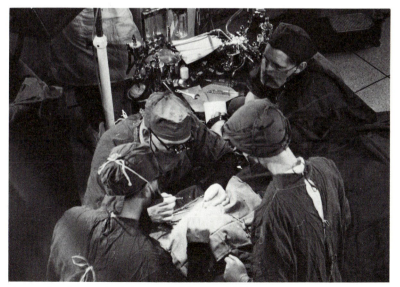

A corneal graft operation being recorded for Your Life in Their Hands

by satellites over the Pacific and Indian oceans to be watched simultaneously by 600 million people.

The Apollo project brought new audiences for the BBC astronomer Patrick Moore; it also brought new status for television's science correspondents, James Burke of the BBC and Peter Fairley of ITV. Burke was later awarded his own series, *The Burke Specials*, in which he dazzled a studio audience with fast talk, experiments and demonstrations of scientific equipment as he presented his visions of the computerised world of tomorrow.

The Ascent of Man, a 13-part BBC2 series by Dr Jacob Bronowski in 1974, was filmed all over the world to present a personal view of the evolution of scientific thought and ranked as an achievement comparable to Kenneth Clark's *Civilisation*.

But the principal regular series in recent years have been the BBC's *Tomorrow's World* and *Horizon*, and Yorkshire Television's *Discovery*, all reporting on the latest scientific advances. The BBC also presents an annual *Young Scientists of the Year* contest in which syndicates from schools show their work on projects of their own choosing. Examples have included a London school's research into the influence of sound on plant growth, and a Leicester school's investigation of the connection between migraine and diet.

Chapter 13

Religion

In the beginning, television had little or no time to devote to religion, for there were only two hours of transmissions on weekdays and on Sundays the screen stayed blank. When Sunday television began in 1938 it was for only one hour a day.

But it was not merely the sparsity of television time that caused religious programmes to be omitted. There was a feeling both in the Church and the BBC that although church services were broadcast on radio, television was not a suitable medium; that the act of worship could be devalued by screening it for viewers who might not be properly attentive or responsive.

It was not until ITV arrived in 1955 that religion achieved its own regular slots – known irreverently as 'God slots' – and then it was granted a privileged place in the schedules quite disproportionate to viewing figures and even to the number of church-goers in the country.

However, over the years since then the nature of religious programmes has changed radically, from parsonic homilies and discussions between churchmen to genuinely questioning programmes justifying by television standards their place in the schedules. At the same time religious programmes have moved nearer to, and in some cases virtually merged with, the mainstream of television.

The holy hour

Nowhere has the change been more marked or more controversial than in the early evening on Sundays. When ITV began, television closed down between 6 and 7.30 on Sunday evenings (except for occasional live outside broadcasts of events of major public interest) in order not to deter church-going.

Though there was no demand from the Church to have religious programmes at this time – and the Church, generally, had opposed the establishing of ITV – Associated Television, then the weekend contractors for London, took the initiative. With the support of the ITA and the Central Religious Advisory Committee, which already advised the BBC on religious matters, and was to do the same for ITV, the company persuaded the Postmaster General to allow the use of the 'closed period' for religious purposes, and in January 1956 introduced a half-hour programme at 7 p.m. called *About Religion*. In the main, it featured prominent Christians.

In 1958, ABC, then the weekend contractors for the North and Midlands, moved in at 6.15 p.m. with a programme called *The Sunday*

Break. Daringly innovatory, it was the brainchild of Howard Thomas, then managing director of ABC. Thomas had two teenage daughters and his house was often filled with young people. This led him to conceive *The Sunday Break* as a programme in which religious questions of interest to teenagers could be discussed in a youth club setting and interspersed with pop music. The first programme included film actress Janette Scott, still a teenager herself at the time; later programmes featured Chris Barber and his jazz band hotting up hymns. One programme had clips of Western films and a discussion on the morality of the Western. When it was asked how religion came into this, an American professor who had been booked to discuss the subject said, 'Everything in life has a religious significance if seen in the right perspective.'

With this philosophy the use of what had become known as the 'holy hour' was widened steadily. Typical programmes asked: could one be a Christian in the army, in sport, in politics, in big business? What was the Christian attitude to gambling, flag days, warfare, smoking? Programmes began to include agnostics, humanists and atheists as well as spokesmen for the Christian churches. By the late sixties, religious programmes were beginning to reflect the interest of young people in Eastern religions such as Buddhism, Hinduism, Zen and the cult of the Maharishi. In 1968 London Weekend's *Roundhouse* televised fierce arguments over religion live as they happened in the North London centre of that name.

Discussion series continue. Recent examples have been the BBC's *A Chance to Meet* in which Cliff Michelmore invited studio audiences to question the famous about their beliefs, and *The Sunday Debate* in which Robin Day chaired discussions on crime, immigration and the distribution of wealth. Granada's *Seven Days* debated the moral implications of subjects in the news, though three programmes in an LWT series called *Private Views*, featuring union leader Clive Jenkins, poet Brian Patten and broadcaster Audrey Russell, were banned from the closed period by the IBA for not having sufficient connection with religion.

However, the holy hour programmes have gone far beyond the simple discussion programme. Early on, ITV screened *Christ in Jeans*, a modern dress version of the Crucifixion, and *A Man Dies*, a rock'n'-roll passion play performed by Bristol teenagers. In 1962 *Journey of a Lifetime* filmed a young couple visiting the Holy Land. More recently there have been write-a-hymn contests, a satirical laugh-in series, hymn requests introduced by disc jockeys and religious quiz shows with questions such as 'Who was the Red Dean?' and 'What did Cain say when God asked him where Abel was?'

In the early years the holy hour had been switch-off time: viewing figures dropped when it began and rose again when it ended. Then in 1961, the BBC introduced *Songs of Praise*, an ecumenical 'sacred concert' in which people from a variety of churches in a district gathered in one venue to sing familiar hymns. Cameras roved over the architecture and the faces of the congregation, and the viewing audience rose gradually to four million, which made the series more popular than *Grandstand*, the BBC Saturday afternoon sports programme.

In September 1969 Jess Yates, a Yorkshire Television producer, topped *Songs of Praise* with *Stars on Sunday*. He blended popular hymns and show business, bringing big and unexpected names to the show. Harry Secombe sang *Ave Maria*; the Bachelors sang *You'll Never Walk Alone*; Dame Anna Neagle, James Mason and Raymond Burr took turns with Cardinal Heenan and the Archbishops of Canterbury and York in reading from the Bible. Yates gathered the famous from every walk of life – Gracie Fields and Lovelace Watkins, Prime Minister Edward Heath and Earl Mountbatten of Burma – and the settings were lavish enough for a Liberace spectacular. The programmes reached fifteen million viewers, becoming the first religious series to enter the Top Twenty charts, and this at a time when churchgoing was declining. Fan mail and request letters numbered 5,000 a week, and yet many Christians were not entirely happy, nor was the IBA; the programmes were thought too sentimental, too cosy, too show-biz. They were later toned down.

But they caused other companies to reconsider the religious slot. In 1972 Granada began *Adam Smith*, a long-running drama series about a parson struggling to help his parishioners with their various problems, while wrestling with his own doubts and uncertainties following the death of his wife. It was the same sort of formula as *Dr. Finlay's Casebook* and other drama series, but translated to a church background. (In fact, Scottish Television showed it on a weekday.)

In January 1972 the closed period ended officially when Minister of Posts and Telecommunications Christopher Chataway (the former ITN newscaster) withdrew governmental restrictions on hours of broadcasting. The BBC and ITV said promptly that they were in no hurry to change the pattern of viewing at that time, though television's religious advisers had been divided in their attitudes to the holy hour for many years. Some saw the end of the closed period as a further step in the secularisation of Sunday; others felt that it might be for the best, that religious programmes need no longer constitute a ghetto on Sundays but could find their own slots in the schedules according to merit. In fact, some of the most effective and most viewed religious programmes of recent years have been put out, not in religious time, but at peak periods, by other departments. For example, ATV's *Go,*

Go, Go with Arthur, a documentary on the visit to Birmingham of American evangelist Arthur Blessitt; the Thames documentary, *The Making of a Saint*, on the process of canonising Pope John, and Dennis Potter's BBC play *Son of Man*, which starred Colin Blakely as Jesus. By 1976 the end of the holy hour was near.

Epilogues and church services

Changes have also taken place in religion's two other main areas of television – the Sunday morning service and the week-night epilogue. At the start of ITV in 1955 the programme companies introduced an epilogue immediately before closedown. It was originally a simple homily spoken to camera by a parson from the region.

These epilogues soon revealed, if nothing else, that many of the clergy were atrocious broadcasters and the ITV companies began coaching courses for them at which they learned to drop their pulpit manner for a more homely style better suited to television. Similar courses (predecessors of the kind since utilised by politicians and industrialists) have continued and the interdenominational Churches' Television Centre at Bushey, Hertfordshire, and the Catholic Radio and Television Centre at Hatch End, Middlesex, have developed their own.

In the meantime the nature of the epilogue has changed. Around 1963 *The Epilogue* fell into disfavour as a title and was replaced by a variety of new ones, among them *The Last Programme*. Book and film reviews with a Christian viewpoint were introduced; there were mini-documentaries and discussions, even a comedian cracking gags about the seven deadly sins. In some areas the short, nightly programmes yielded to longer, less frequent ones, and no longer do they invariably go out last thing before bedtime. Tyne Tees developed a breakfast-time *Prologue*, complemented by a Bible reading on sound only at closedown. Border introduced regular religious spots into its magazine programme *Lookaround*, and Thames included them from time to time in *Good Afternoon* and *Today*. Ulster instituted a five-minute religious view after Monday's *News at Ten*. Yorkshire, Granada and HTV have never transmitted epilogues.

Even the Sunday church service has altered. When ITV started there was no television until after lunchtime on Sundays but in 1957 ITV introduced a morning service, the first being a Battle of Britain drum-head service from the RAF station at Biggin Hill.

ITV still continues weekly Sunday morning services (although they are shown less frequently in Scotland), but in 1972 they were moved to an earlier time to accommodate *Weekend World*, a current affairs series, and many services have been experimental in form and televised from a studio. The BBC now shows a church service only fortnightly, alternating services with *Seeing and Believing*, which is usually located in a church but incorporates religious discussion and sometimes music, drama and dancing.

Chief advisers to both the BBC and ITV on policy and the allocation of programmes between the various denominations remain the Central Religious Advisory Council, whose current chairman is the Bishop of St. Albans, but on which all the main Christian churches are represented. In addition, the IBA and each of the fifteen ITV companies have their own panels of religious advisers to help on day-to-day programming. The BBC has a complete religious department, most of whose staff are ordained.

Chapter 14
Regional programmes

Most of the programmes mentioned in this book have been networked ones, shown throughout the country, but television also provides programmes for viewers in individual regions, designed to reflect the special interests of those areas.

The leader in this direction has been ITV. BBC television was born and bred in London and the capital has remained its headquarters for programme making and scheduling. After television spread into Scotland, Wales and Northern Ireland the BBC began to provide locally made programmes for viewers in those regions, but until 1970 it had only three English regional centres – Birmingham, Bristol and Manchester.

ITV on the other hand was planned from the start on a regional basis with the country divided into areas served by independent programme companies. In the sixties the BBC recognised the dual merits of this system, which adds variety and individuality to the national network and also enables viewers to see programmes tailored specially for their locality.

BBC regions

So in 1970 there was a reorganisation. The regions of Scotland, Wales and Northern Ireland were retained and the three English regions were increased to eight. The existing regional centres in Birmingham, Bristol and Manchester were designated network production centres and charged with producing a proportion of programmes for the whole country as well as local programmes. At the same time five new regional centres were established at Norwich, Leeds, Newcastle upon Tyne, Southampton and Plymouth to produce purely local programmes in the manner of ITV's smaller companies.

Since then there have been suggestions inside the BBC that the number of regions should be increased by such additions as Merseyside, Humberside and Cumberland. But the number of regional variations from the networked schedule has remained small compared to that within ITV, and control of finance, senior staff appointments, staff training etc. has remained with London.

The policy and content of the Scottish and Welsh programmes shown within those regions have been controlled since 1964 by two National Broadcasting Councils. (Northern Ireland, like the eight English regions, has an advisory council.) The Scottish region, based on Glasgow, has made the biggest contribution to the network of the three national regions with such drama programmes as *The View from Daniel Pike* (a private detective series), *Scotch on the Rocks* (a thriller serial) and *Weir of Hermiston* (a serial based on Robert Louis Stevenson's novel). There have also been local light entertainment shows featuring such artists as Moira Anderson and Kenneth McKellar. The Welsh service, based on Cardiff, and the Northern Irish, based on Belfast, produce mainly local programmes, the Welsh output of twelve hours a week including seven hours in the Welsh language.

In England the Birmingham network centre's production ranges from *Pot Black* snooker tournaments to programmes for immigrants. Manchester specialises in quizzes and games like *A Question of Sport*, *Call My Bluff* and *The Movie Quiz*. Bristol specialises in natural history programmes including *Web of Life*, *Look Stranger* and *The World About Us*. These three centres are also responsible for the local productions for the Midlands, North-West and West regions respectively. The chief local programmes of these three and the five other regions, East Anglia (Norwich), North (Leeds), North-East (Newcastle upon Tyne), South (Southampton) and South-West (Plymouth) are the weekday news and current affairs programmes, e.g. *Midlands Today* and *South Today*, *Look East* and *Look North*, which are contained within *Nationwide*.

ITV regions

ITV has fourteen regions served by fifteen companies, five of which are charged with producing the bulk of the networked programmes (though they also produce local programmes) and ten whose main responsibility is producing local programmes (though they may also contribute to the network).

Chief architect of this system was Sir Robert Fraser, Director General of the ITA from its creation in 1954 until his retirement in 1970. The Australian-born former newspaper leader writer explained his thinking in these words: *

> For thirty years there had been only one permitted broadcaster in the whole country, centralised, unitary and very large. Once it had been decided that other broadcasters were to be allowed, it seemed suddenly more in keeping with the desirable forms of communications in a free society that the new institutions should be plural and decentralised, taking the form of a group of independent companies, as many as technical and financial limitations would allow.
>
> Then, if there were to be a number of broadcasters to provide the network programmes, it seemed that power and opportunity, as far as they were concerned, should be spread evenly rather than

* Address at Goldsmiths Hall, September 1970.

unevenly, that there should be a balance of equal forces rather than the dominance of one. And, thirdly, it seemed clear that the initial network companies should not all be based in London, that capital of everything, but that television centres should be created in the most heavily populated regions, the North and the Midlands.

Scotland, Northern Ireland, Wales and the regions of England are communities in their own right. The United Kingdom is not London, Manchester and Birmingham. Were they not to play any part in Independent Television save as receivers of programmes, not as producers of programmes? So it came about that the ten regional companies came into existence, one by one, as each proved its viability, taking the network programmes from the network companies, but adding those local programmes, now in total twice the number of network programmes, that are one of the strengths and virtues of Independent Television.

Since this chapter is concerned primarily with regional programmes it is reasonable to list the regions in ascending order of size. The ten ITV regionals, with their viewing populations, the programme companies that serve them and their centres, are as follows:*

Channel Islands (107,000): Channel Television, St. Helier, Jersey.
The Borders and Isle of Man (505,000): Border Television, Carlisle.
North-East Scotland (915,000): Grampian Television, Aberdeen.
Northern Ireland (1·3 million): Ulster Television, Belfast.
South-West England (1·4 million): Westward Television, Plymouth.
North-East England (2·5 million): Tyne Tees Television, Newcastle upon Tyne.
East of England (3·1 million): Anglia Television, Norwich.
Central Scotland (3·6 million): Scottish Television, Glasgow.
Wales and the West of England (3·7 million): HTV, Bristol and Cardiff.
South of England (4·3 million): Southern Television, Southampton.

It was laid down by Sir Robert Fraser that 'A local company is not to be measured by its network scores but by the programmes with which it contributes to the quality of local life.' All these companies produce regional news and current affairs programmes, which are an important part of independent television, and all the regions and companies have distinctive features.

Channel Television, the smallest of the ITV companies and the poorest financially, has a staff totalling only sixty-three and tiny studios, but because of the number of French speakers in the Channel Isles it broadcasts in French as well as English, with *Actualités*, a

* *TV and Radio 1976.*

newscast, *Commentaires*, a current affairs programme, and *Bulletin Météorologique*, a daily weather forecast.

Tyne Tees, situated in an area of high unemployment, includes among its programmes a television labour exchange, *Where the Jobs Are*.

HTV (formerly known as Harlech Television after its chairman Lord Harlech) produces 15 programme hours a week in both English and Welsh from twin studio centres in Bristol and Cardiff. The Harlech consortium, which included notable Welshmen such as Sir Geraint Evans, Stanley Baker and Richard Burton, was allocated the region in 1968 when Television Wales and West was dispossessed of it by the ITA. The Authority thought the newcomer would be better; and it was believed that TWW incurred the Authority's displeasure by concentrating too much of its operation in London.

Scottish Television produces more than 1,000 programmes a year including half-hour plays that have starred native artists such as Roddy McMillan, Robert Urquhart and Fulton Mackay.

Southern Television, with its long waterfront, was unique in owning a 72-foot long power vessel, *Southerner*, which constituted a floating outside broadcast unit for nautical series like *Afloat*. Southern has made a star out of Jack Hargreaves with his country series, *Out of Town*; it has also contributed children's programmes including *Freewheelers* and *How* to the network and has presented opera from Glyndebourne.

Anglia makes a contribution to the network with plays from the drama department, which is headed by John Jacobs, brother of David, and with its *Survival* natural history programmes.

Border, Grampian, Ulster and Westward are all small stations serving the particular needs of relatively sparsely populated parts of the United Kingdom which would inevitably be neglected in a unitary system. The smaller the company, the greater its local involvement.

ITV's Big Five

Continuing upwards in size, the big four regions of ITV, which are served by the big five central companies, are as follows: *

Yorkshire (5·4 million): Yorkshire Television, Leeds.
Lancashire (6·9 million): Granada Television, Manchester.
Midlands (8·2 million): ATV Network, Birmingham.
London (11·5 million): Thames Television, weekdays from Monday to 7 p.m. Friday; London Weekend Television for the remaining time.

* *TV and Radio 1976.*

They all produce local programmes like the minors, but are responsible additionally for most of the networked shows.

Yorkshire Television began operations in 1968 with territory carved off the Northern region which had been entirely Granada's. Its best-known programme is probably *Stars on Sunday*, though it also shows the documentaries of Alan Whicker (who was one of the consortium that founded it) and is particularly strong in drama series like *The Main Chance* and *Justice*.

Granada likes to refer to its region as Granadaland. Founded by Lord Bernstein of Leigh, a Socialist peer, it is one of the most strongly individualistic of the ITV companies, specialising in gritty north country dramas with working class heroes, such as *Sam* and *A Family at War*, and is also responsible for *World in Action*, the documentary series with the approach of a tabloid newspaper. Typically, its local output includes *This Is Your Right*, a series billed as guiding viewers through government and municipal red tape.

The ATV Network is headed by Sir Lew Grade, formerly a theatrical agent, and is best known for variety spectaculars like *The Engelbert Humperdinck Show* and *Sunday Night at the London Palladium*, though Sir Lew is quick to point out that his company produces a wide range of other programmes including some of the most popular documentaries. Sir Lew is television's top salesman, flying regularly between Britain and America to set up deals with American networks on programmes like *The Persuaders* and *This is . . . Tom Jones*, which bring ATV more dollars than are earned by the BBC.

London Weekend Television was another programme company established in the 1968 revolution. It had a troubled early life when financial problems hindered it from fulfilling its original programme plans, and some of its key executives resigned. Rupert Murdoch, the newspaper owner, took a financial stake and John Freeman, the former British ambassador to the United States, who had made his mark in television with his *Face to Face* interviews on BBC, became chairman and chief executive. It produces *World of Sport* on behalf of the network; other programmes include *Weekend World* and *Upstairs, Downstairs*; and in 1975 it introduced *The London Programme*, a regional series explaining the workings of the capital.

Thames, formed in 1968 from a merger brought about by the ITA between the old ABC and Rediffusion companies, is headed by Howard Thomas, a broadcasting executive of long experience who devised the war-time *Brains Trust* radio series. It produces more than 1,200 programmes a year, mainly networked, from *This Week* to *Love Thy Neighbour* and *Armchair Theatre* to *Magpie*, its chief London-only programme being *Today*, a daily magazine programme introduced by Eamonn Andrews. Its series, *The World at War*, was among the most successful of all television programmes.

Advantages and disadvantages

While recognising the costs involved, the IBA has never doubted the rightness of the regional structure. Sir Robert Fraser declared:

> I am convinced that the plural and regional structure of Independent Television is not only democratically right, and that concentrations in the power to communicate in a free society are deadly dangerous; I am also convinced that the outstanding practical success of Independent Television, the attachment to it of much the largest audience of any of the three television services and the programme standards it has achieved, are directly due to its plural and regional structure – to the wealth of talent for which a plural system provides room at all levels, to the continuous internal competition to excel, and to the co-operative strength of all its rich and varied elements.*

Unquestionably, the regional structure has been responsible for much success. *Coronation Street*, for example, though a networked programme and one of the most popular, was a result of Granada being based in Manchester. It is unlikely that it would have been developed by a London-based company.

And obviously it is good that regions should be free to choose the programmes they think will most interest the viewers in their areas and opt out of others. An England football match, for example, will be a big event to football fans south of the border, but a Celtic–Rangers match would be of more interest in Glasgow. On the other hand, regions are big and the football fan in Margate or Dover is rarely grateful when Southern Television shows him a match featuring Southampton; he would sooner watch a London team like Arsenal (for he lives nearer London and has more contact with London) or for that matter a top team like Leeds or Liverpool, for the best is welcomed everywhere. The BBC has had complaints from Welsh viewers about the showing of programmes in the Welsh language when they would have preferred to see the programmes other viewers were receiving at the time.

It is right that ITV regions should be able to vary the times of day at which they show programmes in order to suit local habits and tastes, but if all the companies decide to take a series it is difficult to understand why they sometimes show it at different times on different days and sometimes in different weeks. Viewers in Glasgow and Aberdeen knew the end of Patrick McGoohan's remarkable series *The Prisoner* a

* Address at Goldsmiths Hall, September 1970.

week before viewers in London and Southampton and Carlisle, who in turn knew it a week before viewers in Norwich, who knew it before viewers in Manchester, who by that time had almost certainly read about the ending in a national newspaper or heard about it from friends. In 1974 *Crossroads* was being seen in London six months after it had been shown in Birmingham, due to Thames having dropped the programme and then resumed it in response to viewer pressure. Manchester viewers were almost a year behind, due to Granada being late in starting to show it.

Regionalisation has many advantages – and some drawbacks.

Chapter 15

Advertising

Britain's first-ever commercial was screened at 8.12 p.m. on 22 September 1955, ITV's opening night in London, when an urgent voice announced: 'It's tingling fresh . . . it's fresh as ice . . . it's Gibbs' SR toothpaste!' That commercial is now stored in the National Film Archive as a fragment of television history.

The effect of the commercials that followed was immediate and startling. Viewers displayed as much interest in the commercials as in the programmes. Jingles were whistled, slogans repeated like comedians' catchphrases, cartoons assessed critically. Today commercials are an accepted and unremarkable part of television. They bring ITV an income of £160 million a year, 98 per cent of the network's total revenue, and there are nearly 22,000 new ones every year.

Advertising rates differ greatly between London and, say, Border regions; they also vary according to the time at which a commercial is shown, but the basic rate for a thirty-second commercial fully networked in the evening peak period is more than £10,000. In off-peak time the rate reduces. And many health, safety and welfare announcements are transmitted free of charge as a public service.

Costs of making commercials have been rising rapidly. Union rules require a crew of at least twelve: two cameramen, two lighting and four sound engineers, a director and an assistant director, a continuity girl and a production assistant. A simple commercial involving just a man and a woman in a kitchen may be taped for a modest amount but a scene filmed in the Far East involving a helicopter, a crowd of extras and a team of stuntmen can send costs rocketing. One company spent £10,000 on flying a group of motorcyclists to be filmed on a Caribbean beach, and when a tobacco company sent a film crew and a dozen actors to Hong Kong for a fifteen-second commercial the costs were estimated at £3,000 a second of screen time.

The making of a commercial is only the beginning of the cost to the advertiser. More than £1·5 million was spent in a recent year on the television advertising of Guinness, and a similar amount on Weetabix. More than £1 million each was spent on advertising milk, Ariel, Persil, Daz, Fairy Liquid, Blue Band margarine, Kelloggs cornflakes and the *Sun* newspaper.

'These figures may sound astronomical,' commented an ITV advertising executive, 'but the audiences are astronomical too. An advertiser knows that he may reach up to eight million homes with his thirty-second networked commercial – around twelve homes for every pennyworth of time.'

Commercial breaks

Advertisers are not allowed any part in the production of programmes. They cannot sponsor them or influence programming; their role is restricted to buying time slots from the programme companies in the same way that they buy space in newspapers.

Parliament has never specified the amount of advertising allowed on ITV; it has merely charged the Authority with seeing that the time allotted to commercials 'shall not be so great as to detract from the value of the programmes as a medium of information, education and entertainment'.* The Authority has interpreted this, ever since the start of ITV, by allowing up to six minutes of advertising an hour, averaged over the day's programmes, but with no more than seven minutes of advertising in any hour on the clock. (The latter restriction is occasionally waived by the Authority if it improves programming, but if commercials run for more than seven minutes in any clock hour there has to be a corresponding reduction elsewhere in the day.)

In the early years of ITV there were 'ad mags' in which commercials were woven into a short programme, one of the most popular being *Jim's Inn* which starred the late Jimmy Hanley and his wife Maggie as hosts of a pub. But ad mags were outlawed by Parliament in 1963. Commercials are now allowed only before and after programmes and during clearly defined 'natural breaks' in programmes.

Not all programmes carry internal breaks. The IBA does not permit advertising, for example, in the course of school programmes, religious services or royal ceremonies, or in programmes of less than twenty minutes. Some documentary and current affairs programmes like *World in Action* and *This Week* are also transmitted without breaks. More than half the programmes transmitted in a typical week contain no breaks. Of the others, half-hour programmes commonly contain one break, and hour-long programmes and most ninety-minute feature films two breaks, while longer programmes may have three or more interludes. There are, on average, three advertising intervals an hour.

Stars of commercials

Many stars are glad to appear in lucratively paid commercials. In recent years Michael Hordern and Bernard Braden have been seen in commercials for soups, Andrew Cruickshank for cheese, John Gregson (cigars), Benny Hill (wine), Diana Rigg (soap), Stratford Johns (cat food), Kenneth More (coffee), Jimmy Young (flour), Norman Vaughan (chocolates), Rupert Davies (tobacco) and Roy Hudd (tea bags).

* Television Acts and IBA Act.

Oxo's Mary Holland (right) with Katie Boyle, who has appeared in soap commercials

A number of artists are now best known for their work in commercials. William Franklyn is one; he has starred in series and single-shot plays and panel games but is generally associated with his commercials for Schweppes though they ended in 1974. And Mary Holland is almost totally identified with the role of 'Katie' in the series of Oxo ads. She has been seen since 1959 as the neat, pretty, middle-class housewife, preparing lunch for her mother-in-law or dinner for her husband's American boss with equally happy results, though her clumsy but good-natured husband, Philip, has been played by two actors during this period, Richard Clark, and for most of the time, Peter Moynihan. In 1964 Katie gave birth to a son, who grew to the age of three in the space of a single summer. But Katie is a real person to many viewers; when she came in from shopping in one commercial and put a joint in the oven without first washing her hands, women from all over Britain wrote to her in sternly warning tones.

Other actors, who are wary of becoming too closely identified with characters in commercials, are ready to hire out their voices for them, and a popular pastime for viewers is identifying the owners. One of the most often heard is the rich, deep voice of Patrick Allen, which has plugged the merits of tea bags, petrol, soups, razor blades and a range of other products. Frank Windsor (John Watt of *Softly, Softly*) is another who has made a profitable income from a distinctive voice, while the churchyard tones of Valentine Dyall have been harnessed to the qualities of a denture cleaner, the wheezy voice of James Hayter to a range of cakes, the plummy voice of William Rushton to a furniture polish, and the all-action style of wrestling commentator Kent Walton to soap pads.

Another important ingredient of many commercials is a jingle, a catchy tune or song, and the success story of all time in this field was the Coca Cola theme, written by Roger Greenaway and Roger Cook, which shot to top place in the Hit Parade when recorded by the New Seekers under the title *I'd Like to Teach the World to Sing*.

Commercials often employ top directors of feature films who are happy to earn up to £500 for a day's shooting between major productions. Lindsay Anderson has made commercials for Kelloggs cornflakes, John Schlesinger for Polo mints, Karel Reisz for Lux toilet soap, Joseph Losey for Horlicks and Ken Russell for Black Magic chocolates. For other directors, like Terence Donovan, commercials have been the route to their first films for the cinema.

But all the talent of writers, artists, directors and technicians cannot guarantee the success of an advertising campaign. The classic cautionary story is that of the commercials for Strand cigarettes. A young man in a trenchcoat, hat on the back of his head, roamed the streets by night, a lonely figure beneath the street lamps as he paused to light a cigarette. The slogan was: 'You're never alone with a Strand.' The commercial was a favourite with viewers and with advertising men. It won awards and its theme music was issued on record, but it failed to sell sufficient cigarettes and the brand died.

ITV's Advertising Code

When the setting up of ITV was still the subject of debate, MPs were concerned that the standard of the commercials should not be lower than that of advertising in the Press. In fact, although commercials are at times criticised for a variety of reasons, ITV has led advertising media in laying down standards.

When the network was born the impact of the commercials was greater than anyone had foreseen and a tighter system of controls had to be devised. The ITA (as the Authority was then) evolved them in collaboration with the programme companies and the advertising industry, and set standards that were tougher and more far-reaching than any the advertising industry had known. They reacted on the advertising industry as a whole, so that it set up similar curbs on the activities of its members. But the Authority, which has amended and tightened its rules regularly, still maintains the strictest controls and ITV refuses many advertisements that are carried in newspapers.

There are more than fifty Acts of Parliament affecting advertising in Britain, from the Accommodation Agencies Act to the Weights and Measures Act, and these concern commercials as they do every other form of advertising. There are also Parliament-imposed regulations relating specifically to television, among them a ban on cigarette advertising (imposed in the interests of health)* and a ban on religious and political advertising (imposed to avoid the swaying of opinion by the advertiser with the deepest purse).† So ads for political parties and Moral Rearmament and appeals for the legislation of soft drugs can never appear on ITV, however much space they may occupy in newspapers. Parliament also banned 'excessively noisy or strident' commercials‡ and 'subliminal' advertising, defined as 'conveying a message or otherwise influencing the minds of members of an audience without their being aware, or fully aware, of what has been done'.§ This step was taken before such advertising – using images of brief duration – had, in fact, become anything more than a bogey in the distance.

These rules and others are embodied in the IBA Code of Advertising Standards and Practice, drawn up by the Authority in consultation with its Advertising Advisory Committee and the Minister of Posts and Telecommunications, laying down the general principle that commercials should be 'legal, decent, honest and truthful'. There are more than thirty sections in the Code. They bar commercials that play on fear, exploit the superstitious or offend against good taste or decency. One section is devoted to 'unacceptable' products and services and bans advertising of marriage bureaux, fortune tellers, betting organisations (including football pools), undertakers and private detectives. This is mostly because of the difficulties of establishing which firms are reputable and which are not, but also because of a feeling that it is undesirable to disseminate their blandishments before a mixed, mass audience.

Another section gives the Authority power to check on the validity of testimonials, to satisfy itself that there is no cheating in contests of the 'Can't tell Stork from butter' type, and that women introduced by name as housewives and mothers to bear witness to the effectiveness of a shampoo are, in fact, genuine housewives and mothers.

A special appendix deals with advertising and children. In the interests of safety, the IBA will not permit scenes showing children near unguarded open fires, playing with matches or leaning dangerously from windows. But the most stringent regulations are those relating to medical advertising, the subject of another appendix. Basically, medical advertising is confined, on the advice of the medical profession, to the simplest and safest of palliatives. Words like 'cure' and 'magic' are as prohibited as obscenities. Anti-smoking products, hair

---

* IBA Code of Advertising Standards and Practice, rule 17.

† Rule 10.

‡ Rule 14.

§ Rule 8.

restorers, contact lenses, slimming clinics, pregnancy testing, bust developers and hypnotic treatments are all on the barred list.

From time to time rules are relaxed experimentally. In 1972 the Authority allowed a three-month run of commercials for women's sanitary protection, but a ban was reimposed following research into public reaction after protests from women who were embarrassed or offended by television publicising such a personal matter.

Advertising control

Originally, the vetting of commercials was carried out by specialists within the programme companies. Authority chiefs saw the commercials only when they appeared on screen and, if they then banned one, a great deal of time and money would have been wasted. So in 1959 the Authority set up its own advertising control department and a system of early joint consultation was started.

In the main, the 15,000 local advertisements every year, which are usually innocuous five- or seven-second slides for local stores and services, are still left to the individual programme companies, though they can consult with the IBA if they wish, and are expected to do so if a point of principle is involved. But the 7,000 new commercials from national advertisers each year, which take up more than 90 per cent of advertising time, are vetted at script stage by the copy group of ITCA (the Independent Television Companies Association, a non-profit-making organisation of which all the programme companies are members) in co-operation with the IBA whose Head of Advertising Control is the supreme arbiter on commercials. They have the assistance of independent consultants in many fields, including a Medical Advisory Panel, composed of practitioners in general medicine, pharmacology, chemistry, dentistry and veterinary science, and with 'second opinion' consultants in pediatrics, gynaecology, dermatology, and conditions of the ear, nose and throat.

In spite of the free availability of the Advertising Code twenty out of every hundred commercials are rejected at the script stage because they contravene one of the rules.

After a commercial has been made it is viewed by the ITCA group and by IBA staff on closed-circuit television. They see about thirty a day, checking that presentation, direction, acting, voices and camera work have not introduced any unacceptable elements, and about two in every hundred are sent back for revision before acceptance.

Archie Graham, who was Head of Advertising Control from 1959 to 1974, bore down from time to time on particular types of advertising. He stopped the use of imitations in commercials, such as glass to simulate highly polished wood. Substitutes are allowed now only in exceptional circumstances. He also stripped white coats from the spokesmen for medical products because they implied that the actors were doctors or scientists. White coats must now be kept in the background and company spokesmen identified as such.

Some decisions are based upon fine points. The ITA passed an airline commercial that featured impersonators of Harold Wilson (then Britain's Prime Minister), Lyndon Johnson (then President of the USA), Jomo Kenyatta (President of Kenya), Moshe Dayan (Defence Minister of Israel) and Errol Barrow (Premier of Barbados) discussing holidays in their respective countries because it was good-natured and amusing, but if it had contained political cracks it would have been rejected.

Chapter 16
Television's impact

TV hits church-going.... TV blamed for school swearing....
Violence and TV may be linked, says BBC. ... Children play dirty
'because of TV'. ... TV is 'making British children best-informed in
world'. ... These headlines were culled from a batch of newspapers
within a few minutes. Television is always in the news and everyone
seems to have opinions about its impact and effects. It is blamed and it
is praised and a great deal of research has been done, but much of that
is contradictory.

Audience measurement

The most publicised and continuous research is into the size of
television audiences, largely because this information is vital to advertisers on ITV. Even here there are contradictions: figures quoted by
the BBC and ITV differ, but then their methods differ.

The BBC's Audience Research Department calculates viewing
figures from daily interviews with 2,250 people about the programmes
they watched the previous day. The panel, which varies every day (so
that the BBC questions 70,000 different people a month, 800,000 different people in a year), is selected as representative of the entire
population (except children under five) in terms of age, sex, social class
and geographical distribution.

ITV uses figures compiled by Audits of Great Britain Ltd for
JICTAR (the Joint Industry Committee for Television Advertising
Research). It has a panel of 2,650 homes in the United Kingdom that
can receive ITV, chosen from a random sample carried out yearly.
Each home has a meter connected to its TV set, which records on
paper tape the time the set was switched on, when it was switched
between channels (and which channels) and when it was switched off.
In addition, each household keeps a viewing diary showing in quarter-
hour sections which members of the family were watching at any time.
From the tapes and diaries minute-by-minute viewing figures are compiled.

Although both the BBC and JICTAR show percentage audience
shares, they do not ask the same questions. The BBC provides percentage audience shares in terms of the average *individual*, JICTAR in
terms of the average *household*. The BBC counts the whole population, whether they have sets that receive BBC only, BBC and ITV or
neither. JICTAR counts only households that can receive ITV
reliably. The BBC counts any programme of which at least half was

viewed, while JICTAR works minute by minute. However, the size of an audience is one matter; what viewers think of the programmes is another. Both the BBC and the IBA supplement audience measurement data with research into audience reaction to programmes.

The IBA's principal source of information is a representative panel of 1,000 adults in London, and random postal samples of 2,000 electors in each of the regions outside London. Respondents record in special diaries how much they enjoyed the programmes they chose to watch. From this data an average score or 'appreciation index' is calculated. This provides a simple measure of audience satisfaction and allows comparisons between the reactions of men and women, young and old, rich and poor, and also any changes in audience satisfaction over the run of a series.

Some programmes like *News at Ten* and *Upstairs, Downstairs* have rated highly both in audience size and in appreciation, but many other programmes with comparatively small audiences rate equally highly in appreciation among those who watch them. The converse also occurs. The IBA carried out a special survey in 1973 on the day after an ATV documentary by David Bailey on Andy Warhol, the pop artist and film maker. A member of the public had obtained a temporary injunction from the Court of Appeal that held up transmission of the programme for two months. It was finally shown in a blaze of publicity

Andy Warhol with his double vision of Marilyn Monroe

about its alleged sex, nudity and bad language. The survey disclosed that it had been watched in 7·25 million homes, which was 50 per cent more than would have been expected without the publicity. More than two in three viewers said that they had made a point of watching it because their curiosity had been aroused by the court proceedings, but it received a low appreciation index, and was rated low both for enjoyment and for merit. Yet only one per cent of those who watched it said they had been offended by nudity, one per cent by bad language and none by sex.

The BBC and IBA also carry out opinion surveys from time to time into the public's view of their impartiality on political matters and their observance of good taste and decency. An IBA survey in 1968, when Mrs Mary Whitehouse was campaigning vigorously against programmes to which she objected, showed that: 'Although half the viewing population never sees anything offensive either on ITV or BBC, about one viewer in three sees something unpleasant once a month or more often.' Another survey in 1972 showed that the public had noticed more material that it considered offensive or in bad taste. The reaction was concerned mainly with bad language and vulgarity. Sex received second mention while violence concerned only half the number who complained about swearing.*

Many other organisations and individuals have carried out research into the impact of television – too many to deal with here – but some of television's effects are obvious. In the cinema we see one immediate effect in the number of films like *On the Buses* and *Till Death Us Do Part* that have been translated from the small screen to the large. A walk through any bookshop shows the effects of television on publishing in the range of books linked to television programmes – from *The World at War* to *Star Trek*. (There is more about this in the next chapter.)

A comparison of current newspapers with those of the early fifties shows that the space given to television news and gossip about television programmes has increased enormously, while a less obvious effect upon newspapers has been that, because most people now rely on television for the latest news, the newspapers carry more in-depth background features.

Television commercials must have an effect in creating markets for products, otherwise advertisers would not spend the millions they do on them, and once-esoteric pursuits like show jumping have grown into major sports because of television coverage.

Other effects of television are arguable. To what extent did news bulletins showing piles of rubbish in the streets of Glasgow turn the public against the municipal workers' strike in 1975? How far did

* *IBA Annual Report*, 1973.

current affairs programmes describing old people dying of hypothermia turn the public against power workers in their industrial action? Should television cameras cover protest demonstrations when demonstrators behave differently – or only demonstrate at all – because television cameras are there? How much has television influenced voters at general elections?

Research at the time of the 1964 election showed that the sound was turned down in one in eight households during party political broadcasts, and most people questioned said that the broadcasts had no effect on their voting intentions; they merely reinforced them. Yet television has been accused of influencing voters in some way in every election since.

Politicians have developed new techniques when speaking at meetings where television cameras are present; they have learned to open with a succinct, challenging statement so that it has a good chance of making the news bulletins, rather than including it in perhaps a more logical place later in the speech and risking it being overlooked.

It is a widely accepted part of television and political lore that the Nixon–Kennedy confrontations on American television swung the Presidential election in favour of Kennedy, partly because Nixon sweated profusely. Nixon later did become President, but by that time his advisers had worked on his television image. In fact, one can easily classify television personalities as E (for engaging) or non-E. Non-E's can never command the attention and sympathy that the E's do, no matter how honest or right they may be.

TV and violence

The most arguable question about television's influence is its connection with the increase in violence. In 1968 America's television networks dropped many of their crime series and replaced sound-track gunshots with studio laughter as a sop in the hunt for scapegoats that followed the national horror at the murder of Senator Robert Kennedy. In the search for a simple explanation for all the bloodshed of the preceding years, television programmes, both fictional and factual, were the subject of many attacks.

It was arguable that the crime shows of television were little different from the cops and robbers films shown at cinema matinees thirty years earlier, that when violence erupted in Chicago in the Capone era or when John Wilkes Booth shot Lincoln there was no television. It was easier to blame it than to persuade Americans to give up their guns. In Britain, as in America, television tends to be a whipping boy because of the possibility of real-life violence emulating the violence of the screen.

The theory has been advanced that the screening of a protest demonstration on television results in more demonstrations through-out the land. In America the showing of a film on television in which a maniac planted in an airliner a barometric bomb designed to explode when the plane descended to 1,500 feet resulted in a spate of imitative threats and hoax calls, and the American government asked television stations to stop showing it.

Sir Michael Swann, chairman of the BBC, told the Royal Television Society in 1973, 'As a good many critics have pointed out, the increase of violence has been very much in step with the growth of television and is most marked in those countries that have television. So, at the very least, the connection is a possibility that one must consider very carefully.'

In 1970 the Home Secretary had talks on the subject with the chair-men and directors general of the BBC and IBA, after which working parties were set up and both the BBC and IBA revised the codes on violence that they issue for the guidance of programme makers.

The introduction to the ITV code sets out firstly to answer the question why violence needs to be shown on television at all. It points out that the real world contains much violence in many forms and that when television seeks to reflect the world, in fact or in fiction, it would be unrealistic and untrue to ignore its violent aspects.

This is the ITV code:

All concerned in the planning, production and scheduling of television programmes must keep in mind the following considera-tions: People seldom view just one programme. An acceptable mini-mum of violence in each individual programme may add up to an intolerable level over a period. The time of screening of each pro-gramme is important. Adults may be expected to tolerate more than children can. The policy of 'family viewing time' until 9 p.m. entails special concern for younger viewers.

There is no evidence that the portrayal of violence for good or 'legitimate' ends is likely to be less harmful to the individual, or to society, than the portrayal of violence for evil ends.

There is no evidence that 'sanitised' or 'conventional' violence in which the consequences are concealed, minimised or presented in a ritualistic way, is innocuous. It may be just as dangerous to society to conceal the results of violence or to minimise them as to let people see clearly the full consequences of violent behaviour, how-ever gruesome; what may be better for society may be emotionally more upsetting or more offensive for the individual viewer.

Violence which is shown as happening long ago or far away may seem to have less impact on the viewer, but it remains violence. Horror in costume remains horror.

Dramatic truth may occasionally demand the portrayal of a sadistic character, but there can be no defence of violence shown solely for its own sake, or of the gratuitous exploitation of sadistic or other perverted practices.

Ingenious and unfamiliar methods of inflicting pain or injury – particularly if capable of easy imitation – should not be shown without the most careful consideration.

Violence has always been and still is widespread throughout the world, so violent scenes in news and current affairs programmes are inevitable. But the editor or producer must be sure that the *degree* of violence shown is essential to the integrity and completeness of his programme.

Scenes which may unsettle young children need special care. Insecurity is less tolerable for a child – particularly an emotionally unstable child – than for a mature adult. Violence, menace and threats can take many forms – emotional, physical and verbal. Scenes of domestic friction, whether or not accompanied by physical violence, can easily cause fear and insecurity.

Research evidence shows that the socially or emotionally insecure individual, particularly if adolescent, is especially vulnerable. There is also evidence that such people tend to be more dependent on television than are others. Imagination, creativity or realism on television cannot be constrained to such an extent that the legitimate service of the majority is always subordinated to the limitations of a minority. But a civilised society pays special attention to its weaker members.

This code cannot provide universal rules. The programme maker must carry responsibility for his own decisions. In so sensitive an area risks require special justification. *If in doubt, cut.*

The BBC code is longer and divided into two sections, one covering programmes for children, the other adult programmes.

A BBC Audience Research Department report in 1972 contained an analysis of about a third of the output of BBC1, BBC2 and the ITV London area over a six-month period. The average number of violent incidents per hour was similar for ITV (2·1) and BBC (2·3). Most of the violence was in the news with 10·4 incidents per hour compared with drama (2·0) or documentaries (0·4). Imported American material had more violence than home-produced programmes, and involved death more often.*

In 1973 ITV began a trial in the Midlands region of the use of a small white rectangle on the screen to warn viewers about violent or shocking programmes. The white spot remained in the bottom left-

* *Violence on Television*, BBC.

hand corner of the screen throughout the programme for the benefit
of those switching on late who would have missed the oral warning
preceding the programme. It was used only rarely.

Television as whipping boy

Television's quiz shows have been blamed for inciting avarice, and its
commercials for fostering discontent, materialism and hire-purchase
debts. Its plays have been accused of encouraging drinking, bad language and broken marriages. It has been blamed for juvenile delin-
quency. It has also been accused of increasing cruelty to animals,
damaging eyesight, causing round shoulders and even of harming
children's teeth. (Dentists said that children watch the screen with
their hands against their jaws, leading to deformity and decay, though
many children read that way too.) In fact, television has been blamed
for almost everything except thunderstorms and black spot on roses.

Yet while the current public disenchantment with politicians may
stem largely from their television appearances, it must be at least in
part the fault of the politicians. Likewise, television may have hit the
cinema but that must be due in part to a dearth of films able to draw
the public from their homes.

Such research as has been carried out into television's effects on
viewers tends to be inconclusive, contradictory and out of date, for the
compilation and publication of surveys takes a long time and viewing
fashions change. For example, cash quiz shows have long since ceased
to top the ratings, but the news bulletins can get into the Top Ten.
Night-long viewing of whatever may be on the screen went with the
novelty of television. There is now more selectivity.

One thing all researchers agree on is a need for more research, but
the only thing likely to stop television being an Aunt Sally is the
emergence of a new one, for people have always needed one to throw
things at. There was a time once when many held the opinion that all
the troubles in the world were 'got up by the newspapers'. At different times and among different classes troubles have been blamed on
the motor car, the atom bomb, drink, gambling, Communists,
Socialists and capitalists, but television is the most universal target.

However, there is no longer any snob status to be acquired by
proclaiming, as so many did once, 'We only have television for the *au
pair* and the children,' or 'We have a set, of course, but we only watch
the news and the show jumping.' Television has replaced the weather
as Britain's main topic of conversation.

Chapter 17
Publications

Apart from trade and technical magazines, Britain has two major periodicals concerned with television, *Radio Times* and *TVTimes*. The first carries details of the BBC's television and radio programmes, the second has details of the independent network's programmes. Both are published on Thursday in regional editions, and both sell between three and four million copies. *Radio Times* contains more programme information, while *TVTimes* contains more general-interest articles and more colour pages.

Until 1968 ITV had a number of programme journals in different regions (though *TVTimes* was the oldest and served the greatest number). Then the ITA decreed that there should be a single national ITV programme journal with regional editions. *TVTimes* was re-launched in this role under the joint ownership of all the television companies (except Channel).

BBC Publications, which publish *Radio Times*, also produce the weekly *The Listener*, consisting largely of material from broadcast talks and discussions. Independent Television Publications, which publish *TVTimes*, also produce the weekly *Look-in* for boys and girls with articles and strips based on ITV children's programmes.

Both companies also produce magazine-style 'specials' on major series. The BBC's have included *Dr Who*, *The Onedin Line*, *The Pallisers* and *Shoulder to Shoulder*; ITV's have included *Coronation Street*, *Family at War*, *Crossroads*, *Upstairs*, *Downstairs* and *Edward the Seventh*.

Books

The most valuable works of reference on television are the annual handbooks published by the BBC and the IBA, which cover the activities of the respective organisations during the previous twelve months, and also include comprehensive reference sections. Two recent popularly written books on television are by Peter Black, for many years television critic of the *Daily Mail. The Biggest Aspidistra in the World*, his personal celebration of the BBC's fiftieth anniversary, was published by the BBC in 1972, and *The Mirror in the Corner*, the story of the arrival of ITV and its impact, was published by Hutchinson in the same year.

The number of books of television criticism and analysis is surprisingly small compared with the wealth of books on films and the theatre. Some are based on programme series, many of them supporting

Upstairs, Downstairs – *subject of a 'special'*

adult education series, such as *House of the Future* (TVTimes Family Books), based on a Granada series, and Percy Thrower's *Guide to the Gardener's World* (BBC/Hamlyn), based on a BBC series. Some have been huge sellers: *Répondez s'il vous plaît* (BBC), linked with a French course for beginners, has sold more than 230,000 copies. Up-to-date books on programme production are comparatively sparse but Focal Press publish a range including *The Technique of Television Announcing*, *The Technique of Television Production*, *Factual Television* and *The Work of the Television Journalist*. Her Majesty's Stationery Office publishes official reports concerned with television, and free leaflets and pamphlets on various aspects of television are distributed by the BBC and the IBA. A lengthy list of current publications appears every year in *TV and Radio*, the IBA guide.

For television students

A unique source of information on television is the IBA's Television Gallery, opened alongside its library at its Knightsbridge headquarters in 1968. It is a permanent exhibition with elaborate audio-visual displays on the past and present of television. Two of the most popular exhibits are a twelve-screen presentation on the production of *News at Ten* and a *son et lumière* display on the development of a drama series. Guided tours take about ninety minutes; advance booking is required but this can be done by letter or telephone.

The student of television can also obtain access to many old programmes; the National Film Archive in 1962 began to collect representative programmes for preservation, and now *Callan* and *Hine*, *Bootsie and Snudge* and other heroes of once popular television series live on, never ageing, never dying, cosseted by science in air-conditioned vaults in Berkhamsted. With them, piled on shelves, are tape and film of programmes recording flashpoints in the turbulent history of the times, such as *World in Action*'s coverage of the Grosvenor Square demonstration of 1968. There are historic documentary programmes, such as *Royal Family*, the joint BBC/ITV production of 1969, and also quiz shows and panel games, *Ready, Steady, Go!* and *Stingray*. All are part of television history and the social history of Britain. All will help writers and researchers of the future.

One thing the researcher will notice is that most of the programmes in the National Archive were put out by ITV. The reason for this is that acquiring the programmes usually involves the making of a copy. (The cinema industry produces many copies of a film for distribution but television needs only one film or tape.) Making a copy to the standard sought by the Archive costs money and the bulk of the money available for the purpose comes from ITV, which has been contributing £20,000 a year for the purpose. The BBC does not contribute to the Archive. It maintains its own library, but this was set up for internal use and access to programmes is not as readily available to the outsider as it is at the Archive.

Programmes to be preserved are selected by an unpaid advisory committee of distinguished television critics, programme makers and administrators who meet every two months. The test applied is simple: 'Is there any reason why this programme might be wanted to be seen again?' So a programme may be selected because it showcases the work of a distinguished playwright or designer, or because it shows a moment of history in the making, or merely because it shows some aspect of the changing trends, values, ideals, fashions, obsessions, fancies and absurdities of the age.

Ideally, the Archive would like to be in a position similar to that of the British Museum to which, under the Copyright Act of 1911, it is mandatory to send a copy of every book, periodical and newspaper published in the United Kingdom and offered for sale. Although the Archive could not include every programme, and would not want to, it would like to be offered every programme so that it could select what it wants. However, two attempts to get such a law through Parliament have failed.

Chapter 18

The future of television

The television set of the future will be at least six feet square and may occupy most of one wall in the sitting room. It will provide a choice of twenty-four channels, some specialised and some offering the customary range of programmes, but if these fail to satisfy the viewer he will be able to play a pre-recorded video cassette or video record, or dial a central library and view a programme of his choice. His set will be more than just a provider of entertainment. If he should want to consult an airline timetable, a theatre guide, or even to check his bank statement, he will be able to punch out a code on buttons beneath the set and the information will be displayed on the screen. A housewife will be able to view what is on the shelves at local stores, make a selection from her armchair and order by telephone.

That is a synopsis of some of the more conservative predictions that have been made. None of it is impossible, but most of it must be considered far off at a time when the 625 lines UHF network is still not complete. Yet a great deal of thought has been given already to the provision of more channels and the use of television for data transmission.

Cable television

Not much can be done to increase the number of channels in Britain within the existing system of broadcasting with its internationally crowded airwaves. Facilities are available immediately on the 625 lines UHF system for a fourth channel to be introduced, and an announcement of its allocation can be expected after the Annan Committee's report, but after that no more are likely to be available until the two 405 lines VHF channels are freed – possibly about 1985 – from the obligation of duplicating the 625 lines service in monochrome.

One way of providing more channels that has been the subject of discussion and experiments is by cable. Wired television began in Britain in the early fifties as an extension of the piped radio services that had been operating since before the war. It made headway at first mainly in fringe areas where off-air reception in the home was poor, but now 11 per cent of British homes (about two million in all) receive programmes via cable.

Community aerials used by the cable companies receive signals from the transmitters in the same way as a householder's aerial, but they can be sited in advantageous positions and the signals can be amplified before being piped to homes. Because many more programmes can be carried on a cable than can be broadcast through the air, cable television can provide subscribers with additional programmes such as community news and features.

This became a reality in Britain in 1972 when the Minister of Posts and Telecommunications licensed a company to provide a service in Greenwich offering locally originated programmes as well as BBC and ITV ones. Four more areas – Bristol, Swindon, Sheffield and Wellingborough – were allowed similar experimental services later. And in 1973 the Cable Television Association published proposals for a nationwide service, envisaging nine programme channels linked to every home, the first offering a choice of all locally receivable stations, the others being a citizens' channel on which minorities could air their views, an arts channel, a box office channel for sports and films, a leisure studies channel for education, a local news channel, a shop window channel with advertising, a second chance channel for repeats, and a sound radio channel.

But Sir Robert Cockburn's advisory committee on television technology reported to the government that a national cable network would take up to thirty years to create and cost from £500 million for an eight-channel system to £1,500 million for a twenty-four channel system. The BBC and the ITV companies, while sympathetic to community television, opposed a national cable system on the grounds that it might lead to a deterioration in the present generally satisfactory off-air system. By 1975 four of the five experimental community stations had ceased transmitting and it appeared unlikely that any would ever be viable under the restrictions imposed upon them.

Satellite transmissions

Another possibility that has been the subject of international discussion is transmitting television from a satellite on a fixed orbit in relation to the earth. A problem with the present broadcasting system is that ultra high frequency waves behave like light and, like light, cast shadows when they meet high ground. The 'shadow' areas receive only weak signals and have to be filled in by relay stations. The signal from a satellite, however, falls vertically like the sun's rays at midday and would need no relay stations. This would be of particular benefit to countries like Australia, Canada and India with widely scattered communities. Satellite broadcasting could cross frontiers and bring programmes from various countries within reach of viewers, though not all countries might welcome this. Fears have been expressed that some nations might send up satellites for the primary purpose of broadcasting propaganda, and that there could even be 'pirate television' transmissions of programmes backed by advertising.

Ideally, viewers would be able to receive satellite transmissions directly in their homes by means of small dish aerials on the roofs.

However, a geostationary satellite capable of being received in homes would have to weigh several tons instead of the 200 or 300 pounds of present communications satellites. Smaller satellites would provide less power and community aerials would be required to catch the signal for relaying through a cable network.

A United Nations working group concluded that while broadcasting from satellites to community receivers could be close at hand, direct broadcasting into conventional home receivers was not foreseeable before 1985.

Data transmission

Meanwhile, experiments have progressed in Britain for transmitting data to the television screen. The viewer will be able, by the use of push-button controls, to summon up stock exchange prices, television programme details, a guide to other entertainments, up-to-the-instant news bulletins and weather forecasts, a precision digital clock and other information. He will select the service he wants from an electronic 'book' of up to fifty pages, each containing perhaps a hundred words of constantly updated information on a particular subject. The page selected by the viewer's push-button control will be displayed on his television screen, either against a neutral background or superimposed on the picture being shown.

No new transmitters or frequencies will be required. The information can be carried on the television signal by making use of the infinitesimally short intervals of time between one frame of a picture and the next when no picture information is being sent. This space can be filled by a chain of pulses to convey written information to any suitably equipped domestic set, a complete page of print building up in about one and a half seconds.

Both the BBC and ITV have tried out data transmission systems since 1973, the BBC's being called Ceefax and the IBA's Oracle (for Optical Reception of Announcements by Coded Line Electronics) and they could be put into operation within a short time. All that would be needed would be for manufacturers to produce television sets equipped to receive the information (and adaptors for use with existing sets).

Home entertainment centres

Television sets will continue to become shallower, the objective being 'picture frame' receivers that can hang on a wall. Research is going on into the use of the flat panels instead of cathode ray tubes to make this possible. Before this happens, cordless remote-control station-changing switches are likely to become standard, electronic tuning will improve picture stability, and sound quality will rise to at least 'mid-fi' standard. The switch to colour will continue and the use of video recorders will grow.

After being restricted initially to schools and industry, video cassette recorders became available to the domestic user for the first time in 1974. Also available are pre-recorded video cassettes for playback on television sets. These are expensive but the cassette system has now been joined by a complementary video disc system for playback purposes only. The video disc is a record of standard LP size and material, but carrying a colour programme in its grooves. It can be produced simply and in quantity by the usual pressing technique and more cheaply than a cassette. The more sophisticated players for these discs use a laser beam instead of a stylus or needle and allow pictures to be speeded up, slowed, reversed or frozen as 'stills'.

Furniture in the home will change with the spread of the new equipment. Radios, record players and cassette recorders are already incorporated in combination units and it follows that the television set, radio tuner and video cassette recorder or video record player will become available in one housing to create a luxury home entertainment centre.

There are, of course, people who feel that there is already too much television and that it is impossible to increase the quantity without diluting the quality. That was for years the thinking of many in Whitehall and Westminster, and because of this the development of television has been less rapid than it would otherwise have been. But in less than four decades television has grown from a two-hours-a-day novelty form of entertainment to become the most universal medium of entertainment, information and education the world has known – and it has not finished growing yet.

Bibliography

Some books of the Seventies

The Biggest Aspidistra in the World. A personal celebration of 50 years of the BBC. Peter Black. BBC, 1972.

British Broadcasting. Edited by Anthony Smith. David & Charles, 1974.

British Broadcasting, 1922–1972. A select bibliography. BBC, 1972.

Broadcasting in Britain 1922–72. A brief account of its engineering aspects. K. Geddes. HMSO, 1972.

Day by Day. Robin Day. Kimber, 1975.

A Do You Remember Book: Television. Burton Graham. Marshall Cavendish, 1974.

The Effects of Television. Edited by J. D. Halloran. Panther, 1970.

The Future of Broadcasting. Social Morality Council. Eyre Methuen, 1974.

In and Out of the Box. Robert Dougall. Collins 1973; Fontana, 1975.

ITV Evidence to the Annan Committee. Independent Television Publications, 1975.

The Least Worst Television in the World. Milton Shulman. Barrie & Jenkins, 1973.

The Mirror in the Corner. People's television. Peter Black. Hutchinson, 1972.

Movies on Television. Angela and Elkan Allan. Times Newspapers, 1973.

The New Priesthood. Interviews with programme makers. Joan Bakewell and Nicholas Garnham. Allen Lane, the Penguin Press, 1970.

Radio Times 50th Anniversary Souvenir. BBC, 1973.

The Ravenous Eye. Milton Shulman. Cassell, 1973. Coronet, 1975.

The Television Dramatist. Edited by Robert Muller. Paul Elek, 1973.

Television: Behind The Screen. Peter Fairley. Independent Television Publications, 1976.

Television: Here is the News. Anthony Davis. Independent Television Publications, 1976.

Television: Technology and Cultural Form. Raymond Williams. Fontana, 1974.

The Universal Eye. World television in the Seventies. Timothy Green. Bodley Head, 1972.

The Work of the Television Journalist. Robert Tyrrell. Focal Press, 1972.

Writing for Television in the 70's. Malcolm Hulke. Black, 1974.

A great many free brochures on aspects of television policy, technology and practice are published by the IBA and BBC.

Acknowledgments

The publishers would like to thank the following for permission to reproduce the photographs in this book:

Angle Films Ltd, page 88 (bottom); *ATV*, page 99; *BBC Photograph Library*, pages 13, 14, 20 (top & bottom), 24 (bottom), 26, 52, 76, 77, 78, 81 (bottom), 90, 92 (bottom), 93, 95 (top & bottom), 96, 102, 105 (top & bottom), 118, 119; *CBS Television*, page 17 (top); *Granada Television*, page 79; *ITN*, page 49; *London Weekend Television*, pages 24 (top), 44, 68; *M.C.A.*, page 88 (top); *Popperfoto*, page 59 (top); *Press Association*, page 141; *Roger Scruton*, page 46; *Thames Television*, pages 17 (bottom), 59 (bottom), 61, 66, 81 (top), 92 (top), 107, 110, 113, 116; *TVTimes*, page 148; *Yorkshire Television*, pages 62, 135.

Cover photograph of the set of *Coronation Street* by courtesy of *Granada Television* and *TVTimes*.

Index